Essential Maths

2

Jayashri Bhattacharya

Preface

Mathematics has always been an integral part of human life. From times immemorial, Mathematics has been in our everyday life in various ways irrespective of our knowledge of the mathematical concepts involved in various activities. The school curriculum focuses on the mathematical concepts to cultivate thinking and developing the reasoning skills. It enables the students to take up a systematic approach to solve their daily life problems, aims at exploring multiple aspects of the subject and thus develop a passion for it.

Essential Maths is a series that strives to focus on the maximum involvement of children following an interactive learning pattern. It has been authored by a senior teacher who has been dedicating her years to the teaching of this subject. Following this series will help students to keep away from rote learning and develop their confidence. Their increased confidence and flexibility with numbers will help them handle abstractions and develop logical approach towards the subject. The review exercises help the learners assess their understanding of the concepts. This series also develops the potential of the learners for continuous and comprehensive evaluation, by inculcating the scholastics and co-scholastic skills. Its activity based interactive style will sharpen the learners' minds and make learning enriching and joyous. The books are beautifully illustrated which adds to the overall appeal of the series.

From the Author

Mathematics has always been an integral part of human life. We use mathematics in our everyday life in various ways without being aware of our knowledge of the mathematical concepts involved in the activity. School curriculum includes the study of Mathematics in order to focus on mathematical concepts which help to cultivate the thinking and reasoning skills. It is a systematic approach to enable students to solve their daily life problems. It also aims to allow the students to explore the multiple aspects of the subject and develop a passion for it.

The lab activities and exercises can be used by the teachers as a demonstrative tool in the Maths Lab.

Objectives of teaching Mathematics are:

- To develop an ability to think and reason mathematically
- To handle abstractions
- To cultivate a positive attitude towards mathematics following an interactive learning pattern to help the teacher ensure maximum involvement of the learners
- To increase confidence and flexibility of the learners when numbers are concerned
- To discourage rote learning
- To develop logical sense along with a passion for the subject

The series **Essential Maths** is a carefully graded series prepared in accordance with the new syllabus prescribed by the NCERT on the basis of CCE (Continuous and Comprehensive Evaluation). A remarkable feature of this series is that all the exercises are formed in such a manner that they begin with easy exercises and gradually progresses to difficult ones. The books are activity based and extensive drilling with integrated revision exercises form its key feature. All the books are full of colourful illustrations which make learning a joy! They also inculcate scholastic and co-scholastic skills in the learner.

I take this opportunity to thank a few people who have helped me write this series. They are Ms Seema Chawla my editor for continuously guiding me, my friend Ms Tapasi (Managing Editor, B Jain), my parents-in-law for encouraging me and Aurobindo, my husband, for being very supportive. Heartfelt thanks to Sofia and Shantanu, my kids. Without their suggestions and criticism, I would not have been able to undertake and complete this project.

Jayashri Bhattacharya

Contents

Things We Know

1

Colour the dress of the child on the swing in green.

Draw 2 birds on the tree and colour them blue.

Colour 8 flowers in yellow and 4 flowers in pink.

Colour grass under the tree green.

Colour the bench which is near the tree in purple.

Write the numbers for the following number names.

Seventy one	–	________	Eighty	–	________
Sixty three	–	________	Twenty eight	–	________
Fifteen	–	________	Forty four	–	________
Thirty	–	________	Fifty one	–	________
Sixty	–	________	Sixty five	–	________
Thirty four	–	________	Seventy six	–	________

Write the following in expanded form.

34	=	3	tens	+	4	ones
27	=		tens	+		ones
13	=		tens	+		ones
85	=		tens	+		ones
79	=		tens	+		ones
60	=		tens	+		ones
90	=		tens	+		ones

Circle the largest number in each of the following rows.

48	39	56	80	66	79
9	79	39	69	74	43
64	86	46	66	55	60
52	25	43	34	75	50

Fill in the numbers in the following grid.

1			4						10
		13							
					26				
	32								
				45					
51						57			
		63							70
			74					79	
							88		
91									100

2-Digit Numbers (upto 99)

2

If you are given 15 sticks you bundle 10 of them.

15 ones | 1 ten | 5 ones

If there are 28 beads.

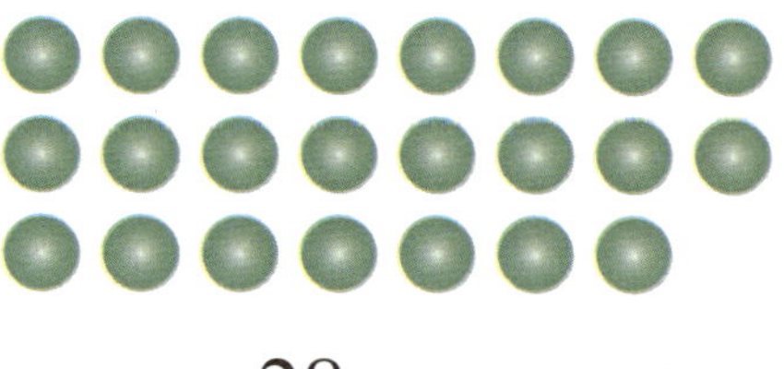

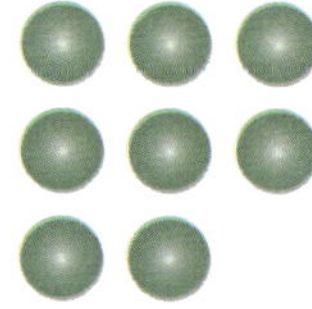

28 ones | 2 tens | 8 ones

So, when you have 10 ones you always bundle it or string it.

Let us look at these numbers and write in the same manner.

4 tens 3 ones	=	40	+	3	=	43
2 tens 7 ones	=	20	+	7	=	27
6 tens 2 ones	=					
8 tens 4 ones	=					
9 tens 7 ones	=					
1 tens 8 ones	=					
3 tens 0 ones	=					
5 tens 6 ones	=					

Abacus

Numbers like 11, 45, 38, 98 are 2-digit numbers. They can be shown on an abacus having two sticks. (for tens and ones respectively)

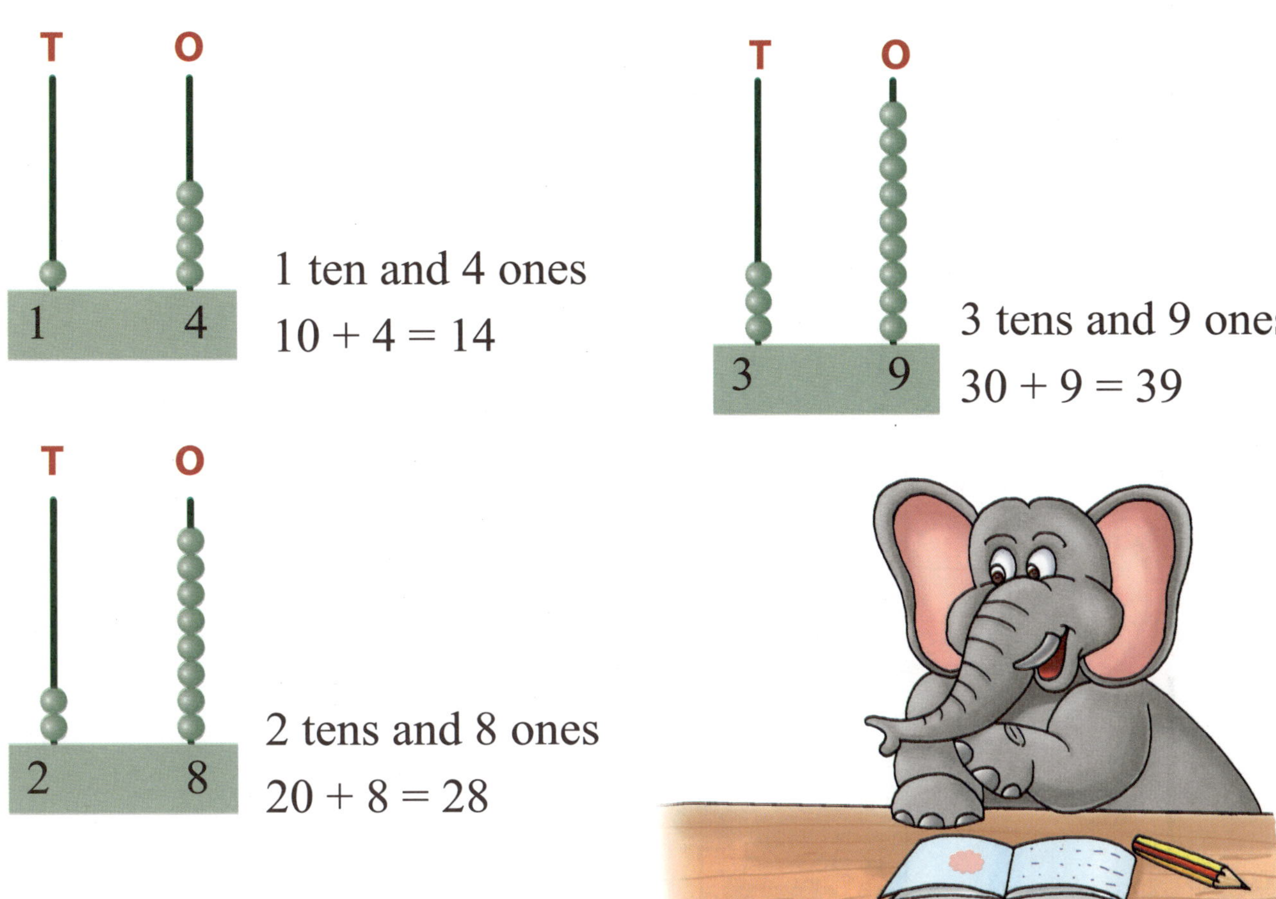

1 ten and 4 ones

10 + 4 = 14

3 tens and 9 ones

30 + 9 = 39

2 tens and 8 ones

20 + 8 = 28

If you have only 10 beads then what will you do to show on the abacus?

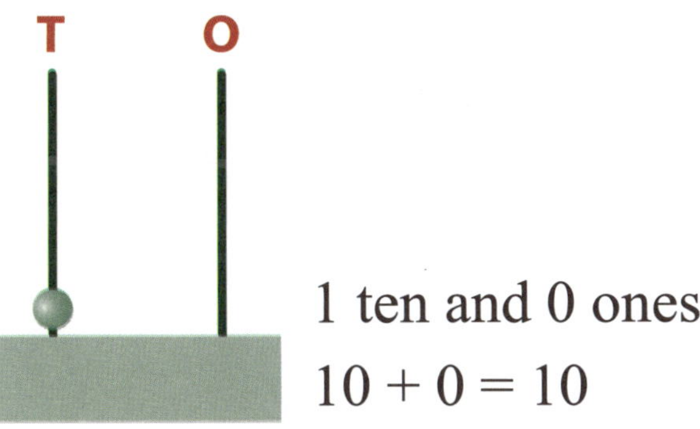

1 ten and 0 ones

10 + 0 = 10

Each stick in an abacus cannot take more than nine beads, as it represents numbers 0 to 9.

Count the beads displayed on the abacus. Fill in the boxes and write the numbers.

3 tens + 3 ones = 33

☐ tens + ☐ ones = ☐

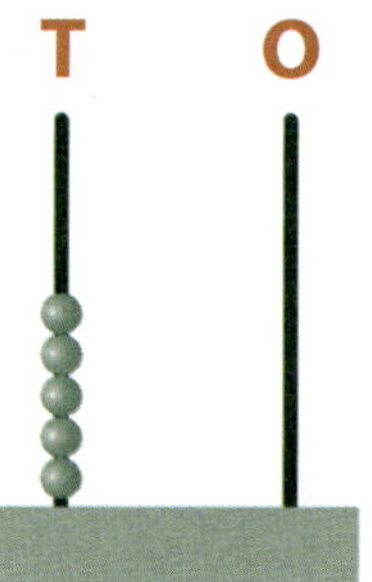

☐ tens + ☐ ones = ☐

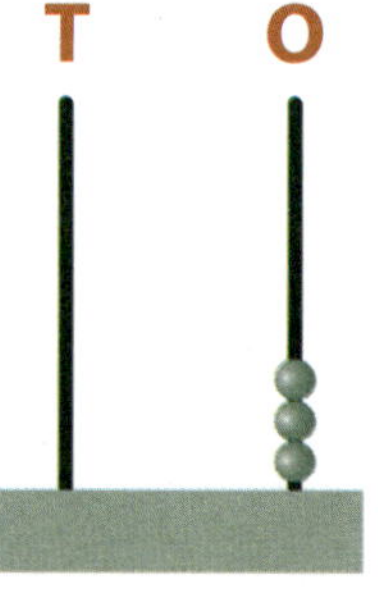

☐ tens + ☐ ones = ☐

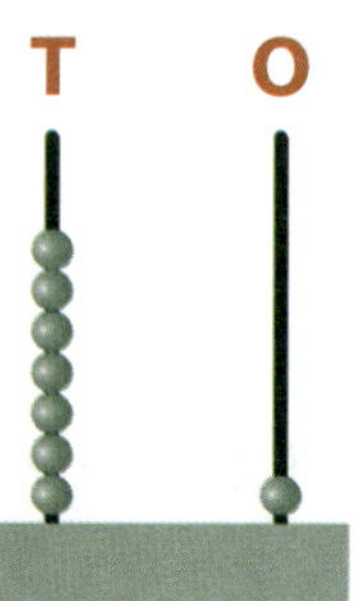

☐ tens + ☐ ones = ☐

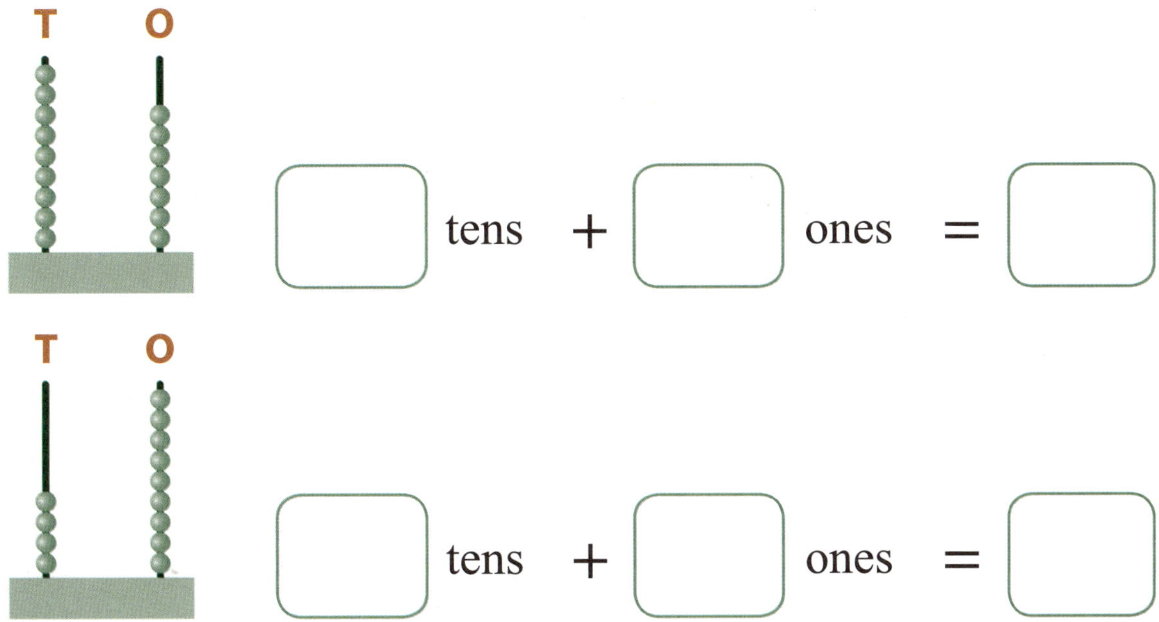

Show the numbers on the abacus by drawing beads on the tens and ones sticks.

T O 18

T O 50

T O 79

T O 45

T O 7

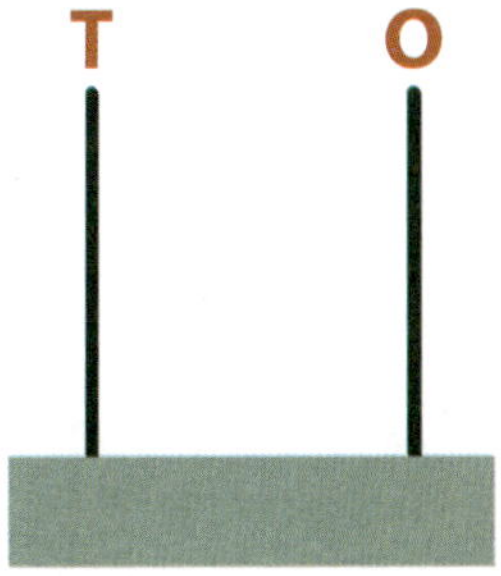

T O 30

T O 21

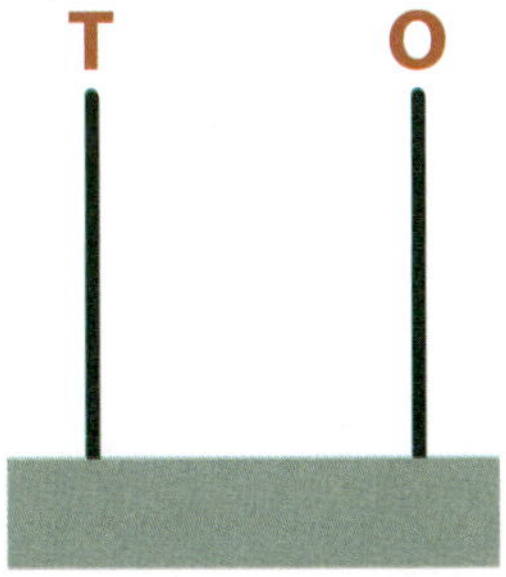

T O 66

T O 97

Complete the following boxes to show the expanded form.

50 + 3 = ☐

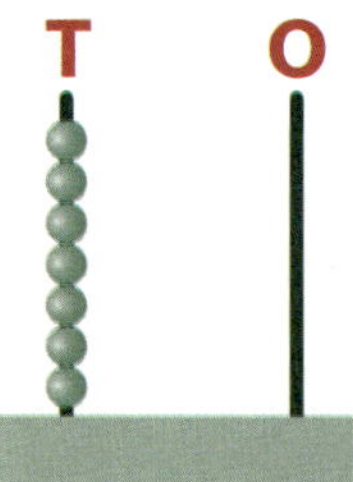

70 + 0 = ☐

☐ + ☐ = ☐

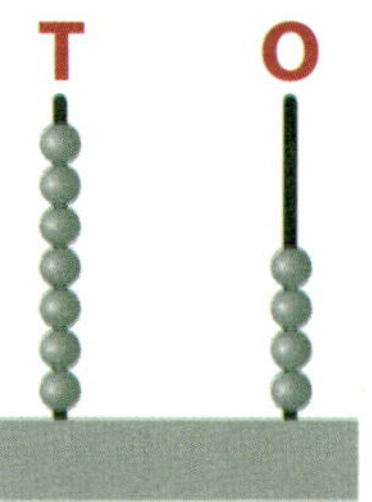

☐ + ☐ = ☐

☐ + ☐ = ☐

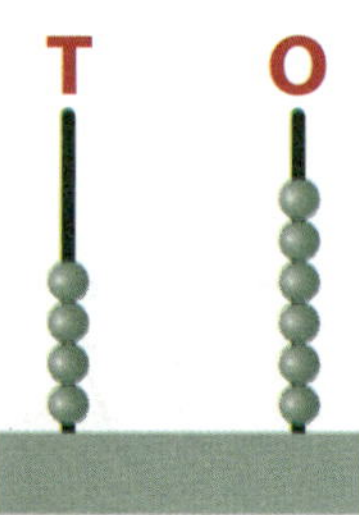

☐ + ☐ = ☐

Place Value (2-Digit Numbers)

EXAMPLE

Write the place value of the digits in the numbers 43 and 56.

T O

43

4 3

Place value of 3 is 3 ones or 3

Place value of 4 is 4 tens or 40

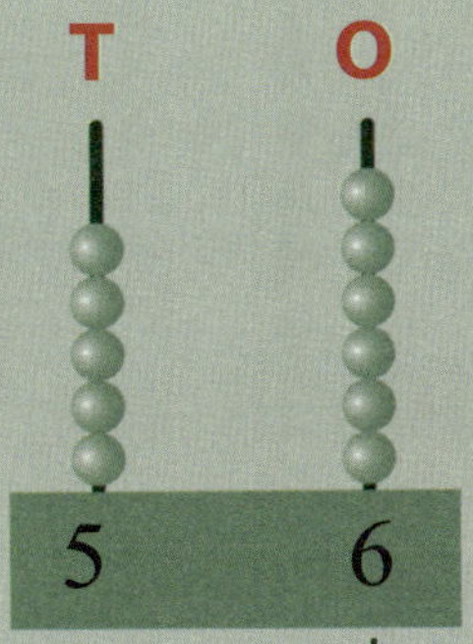

T O

56

5 6

Place value of 6 is 6 ones or 6

Place value of 5 is 5 tens or 50

Now let us see the place value of

2 in 25

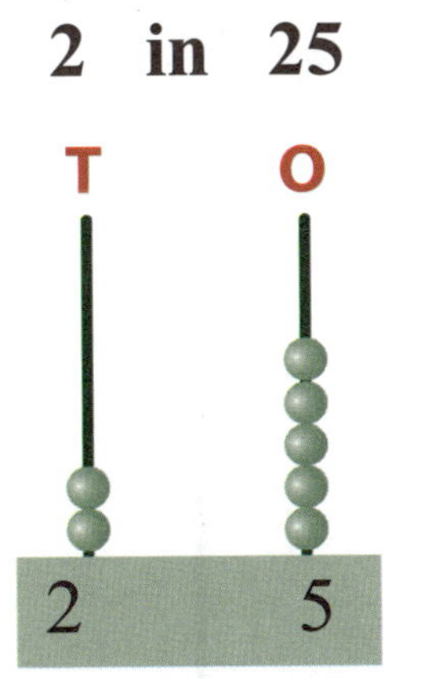

Place value of 2 is 2 tens or 20

6 in 60

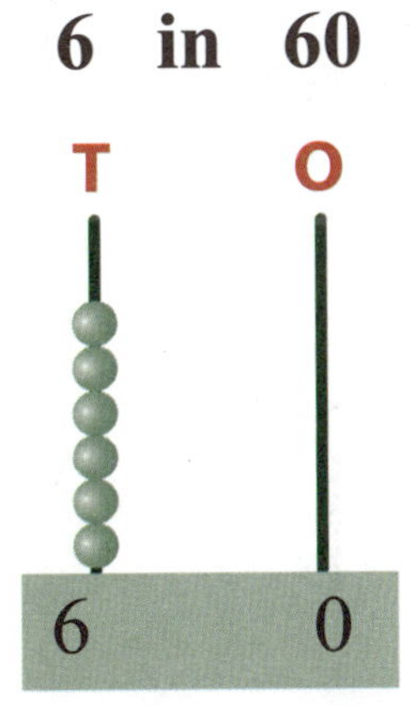

Place value of 6 in 60 is 6 tens or 60

Write the place value of the digits in the boxes.

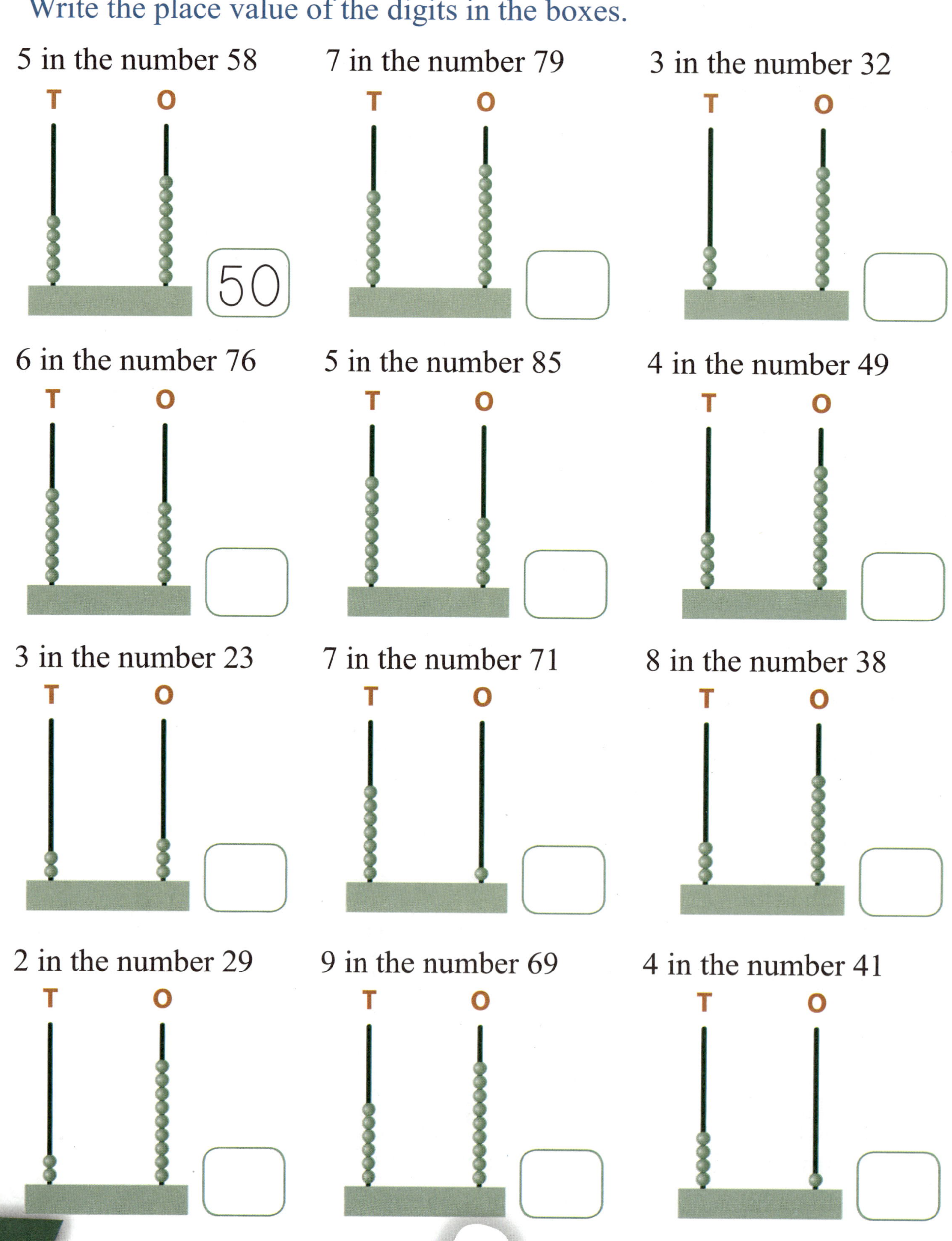

Write the place value of the underlined digit in the box.

T	O		
$\underline{7}$	2	is	☐
$\underline{6}$	4	is	☐
$\underline{1}$	9	is	☐
2	$\underline{0}$	is	☐
$\underline{3}$	1	is	☐
6	$\underline{6}$	is	☐
$\underline{8}$	9	is	☐

T	O		
3	$\underline{8}$	is	☐
8	$\underline{4}$	is	☐
$\underline{4}$	6	is	☐
7	$\underline{5}$	is	☐
4	$\underline{9}$	is	☐
$\underline{7}$	8	is	☐
$\underline{9}$	0	is	☐

Teacher should encourage students to write T, O above the digits.

Write numbers in standard form in the boxes provided below.

40	+	3	=	43
90	+	8	=	
20	+	9	=	
50	+	0	=	
60	+	2	=	
50	+	6	=	
40	+	4	=	

80	+	7	=	
30	+	1	=	
10	+	8	=	
70	+	6	=	
20	+	4	=	
30	+	3	=	
70	+	7	=	

Before, After and Between Numbers

What comes before the number?

☐ 31	☐ 84	☐ 60
☐ 53	☐ 17	☐ 2
☐ 89	☐ 42	☐ 26

What comes after the number?

28 ☐	39 ☐	99 ☐
60 ☐	89 ☐	78 ☐
10 ☐	51 ☐	84 ☐

What comes between the numbers?

59 ☐ 61	28 ☐ 30	38 ☐ 40
11 ☐ 13	49 ☐ 51	60 ☐ 62
50 ☐ 52	26 ☐ 28	81 ☐ 83
34 ☐ 36	19 ☐ 21	75 ☐ 77

Comparing Numbers

EXAMPLE

Compare 34 and 9

9 is a one digit number and 34 is a two digit number.

34 is greater than 9

34 (>) 9

Compare 25 and 58

Write 'O' and 'T' above the digits.

TO	TO
25 has 2 tens	58 has 5 tens

2 tens < 5 tens

So 25 < 58

Greater than '>'; smaller than '<'; equal to '='. Pointed side < is towards the smaller number

Let us compare 72 and 79

TO	TO
72	79

Both have 7 tens

9 ones > 2 ones.

So 72 < 79

When we compare 2 numbers if the digit in tens place is same, then we go to ones place

Compare and fill in the boxes with > or < or '='

67 ◯ 29	30 ◯ 50	20 ◯ 18
86 ◯ 68	54 ◯ 95	37 ◯ 73
41 ◯ 41	65 ◯ 56	91 ◯ 89

Understand the patterns and complete the following rows.

20	21	22	23	24	25	26	27	28
84	86	88	90	92				
1	3	5	7	9				
12	14	16	18	20				
20	30	40	50	60				
25	27	29	31	33				
10	9	8	7	6				
20	18	16	14	12				

Lab Activity

Give two cards with one digit written on each to a group of 2 students. Ask them to make 1-digit and 2-digits numbers.

4	8	→	4	8	48	84
0	5	→				
3	1	→				
7	9	→				
8	6	→				

Position

First	Second	Third	Fourth	Fifth	Sixth	Seventh	Eighth
1st	2nd	3rd	4th	5th	6th	7th	8th

Yellow triangle is 6th

________ square is 4th

________ rectangle is 8th

Fill in the boxes.

In the word **BURGERS**

1. E is the ☐ letter.
2. The seventh letter is ☐
3. The word's first letter is ☐
4. The letter R is at the ☐ and ☐ place.

Write the smallest and largest of each group.

	 **Smallest**	 **Largest**
26, 44, 15, 80	 15	 80
3, 95, 55, 35		
40, 80, 70, 20	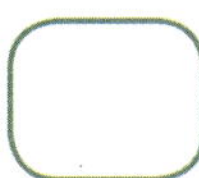	
28, 38, 68, 58		
71, 75, 78, 70		

Write in the ascending order (Smallest to greatest)

17,	83,	67,	71	17	67	71	83
21,	25,	19,	17				
50,	38,	83,	5				
82,	62,	22,	12				
86,	80,	8,	18				

Write in the descending order (Greatest to smallest)

34,	41,	14,	53	53	41	34	14
17,	71,	23,	32				
90,	49,	61,	76				
86,	68,	38,	83				
20,	40,	15,	45				
38,	88,	18,	8				

Addition

3

Addition means putting together. We use '+' sign for addition.

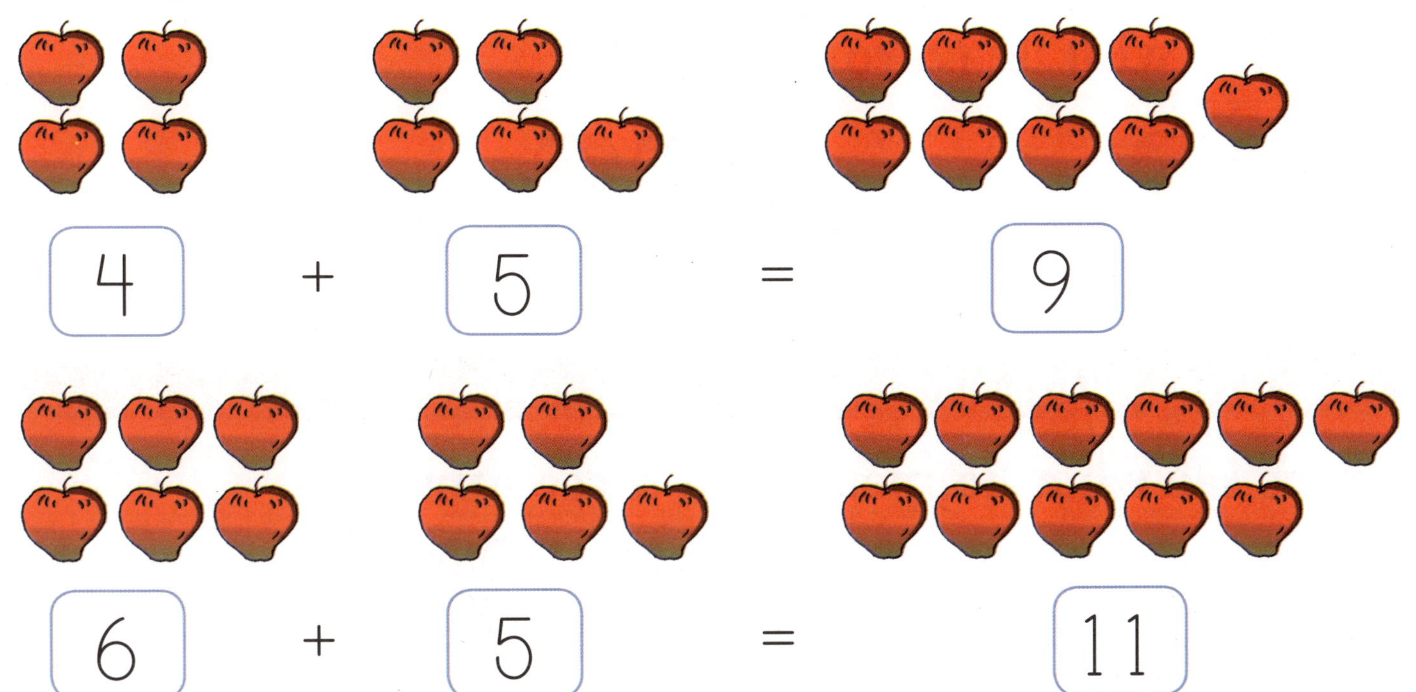

Addition can also be done by counting forward.

7 + 5 = 12

When we add two numbers, we get the **sum**.

Fill in the boxes

6	+	4	=		3	+		=	10	7	+	6	=	
5	+	8	=			+	0	=	9	10	+		=	15
	+	1	=	9	2	+	8	=		16	+	4	=	
9	+		=	15	13	+	2	=		7	+	9	=	

Properties of Addition

2 + 7 = 9 | 7 + 2 = 9

3 + 5 = 8 | 5 + 3 = 8

When two numbers are added in any order, the sum remains the same.

Addition with '0' (zero)

3 + 0 = 3

When 0 is added to a number, the sum is the number it self.

Let us see what happens with three numbers.

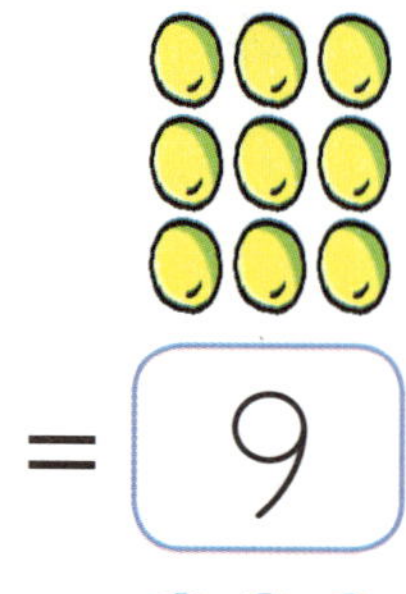

3 + 2 + 4 = 9

4 + 3 + 2 = 9

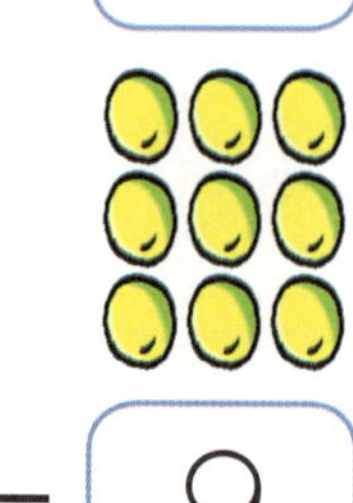

2 + 4 + 3 = 9

Sum remains same, whatever is the order of the same numbers.

Sum of numbers is the same; any of the numbers can be written first.

2 + 3 = ☐ = 3 + 2

7 + 5 = ☐ = 5 + ☐

6 + 5 = ☐ = ☐ + 6

9 + ☐ = 9 = ☐ + 9

9 + ☐ = 9 = ☐ + 9

11 + ☐ = 16 = 5 + ☐

Fill in the boxes

1 + 2 + 3 = 6 = 3 + 2 + 1

6 + 7 + 10 = ☐ = 10 + 6 + ☐

3 + 5 + 6 = ☐ = 3 + ☐ + ☐

0 + 9 + 2 = ☐ = ☐ + 9 + ☐

8 + 4 + ☐ = ☐ = 4 + 2 + ☐

4 + ☐ + ☐ = 15 = 5 + ☐ + ☐

Lab Activity

Students can be given the abacus for performing addition. Abacus can be made as a group activity using erasers, toothpicks and beads. The teacher can demonstrate this addition.

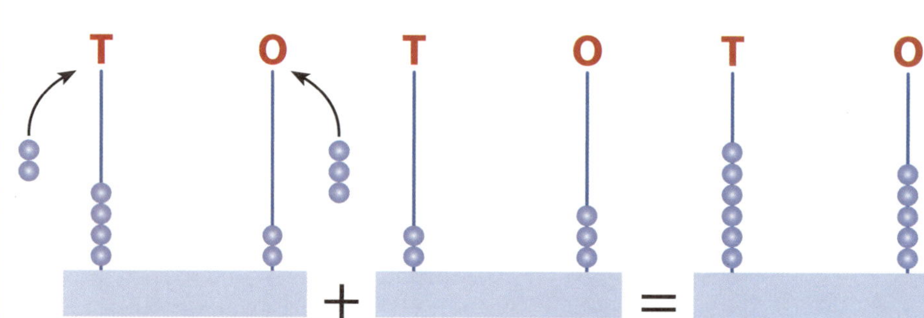

36 +21 ____	85 + 4 ____	76 +10 ____
55 +44 ____	34 +53 ____	60 +36 ____
27 + 51 ____	49 +50 ____	35 +53 ____
42 +47 ____	36 +32 ____	40 +19 ____

Few more using the abacus

T	O
3	8
+ 2	0
+ 1	1

T	O
1	1
+ 2	0
+ 3	8

T	O
2	0
+ 1	1
+ 3	8

T	O
7	9
+ 1	0
+ 1	0

T	O
1	0
+ 7	9
+ 1	0

T	O
1	0
+ 1	0
+ 7	9

T	O
2	3
+ 4	4
+ 1	1

T	O
2	3
+ 1	6
+ 3	0

T	O
4	1
+ 1	1
+ 2	3

T	O
6	0
+ 3	5
+ 1	4

T	O
3	5
+ 1	4
+ 6	0

T	O
1	4
+ 3	5
+ 6	0

Addition by Regrouping

Show 9 + 1 on an abacus.

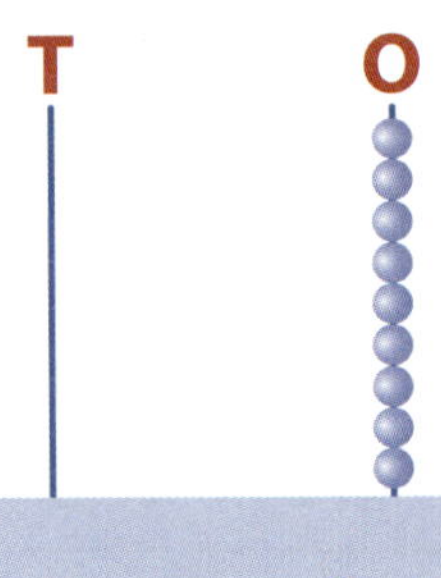

A stick of the abacus cannot have more than 9 beads.

So 9 + 1 = 10 is shown as

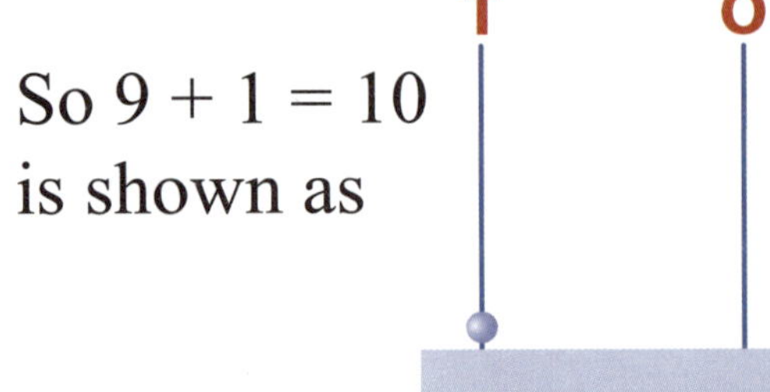

Add 5 + 7 = 12

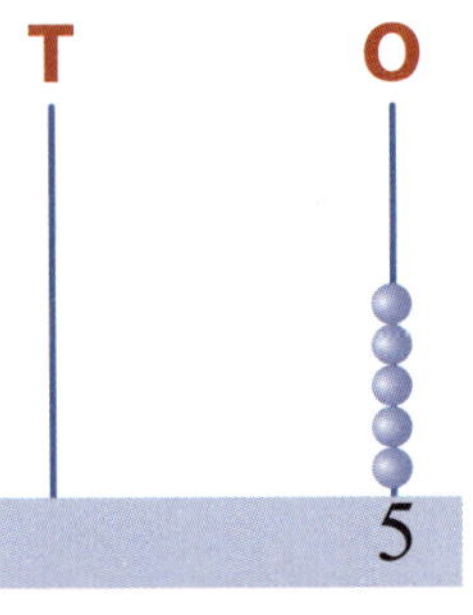

+

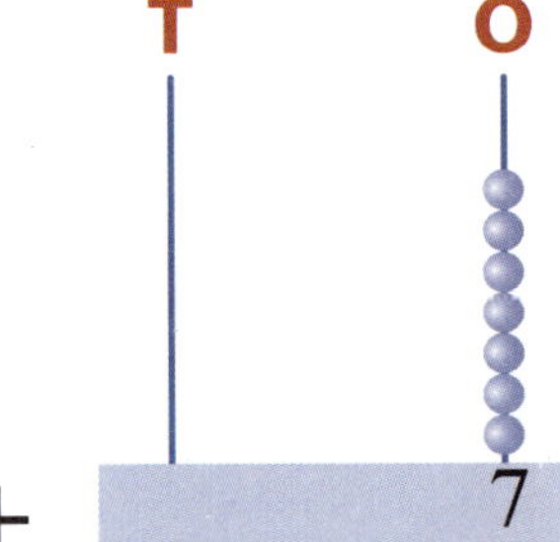

=

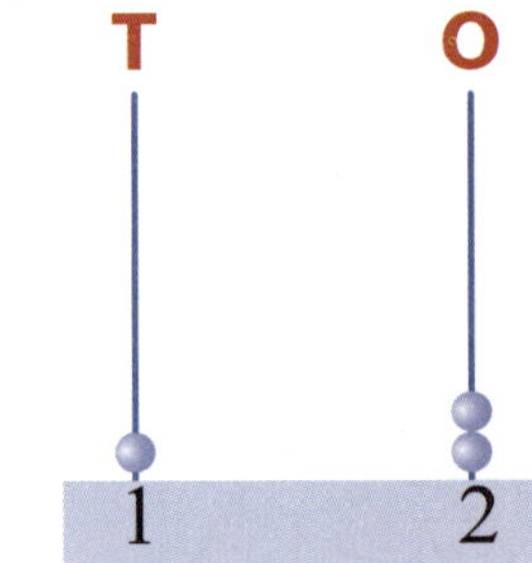

5+7=12

Add

T O	T O	T O	T O
8	9	6	5
+ 5	+ 6	+ 7	+ 6
____	____	____	____

T O	T O	T O	T O
2	4	9	3
+ 9	+ 8	+ 9	+ 7
____	____	____	____

Addition with carrying over

26 + 17 =

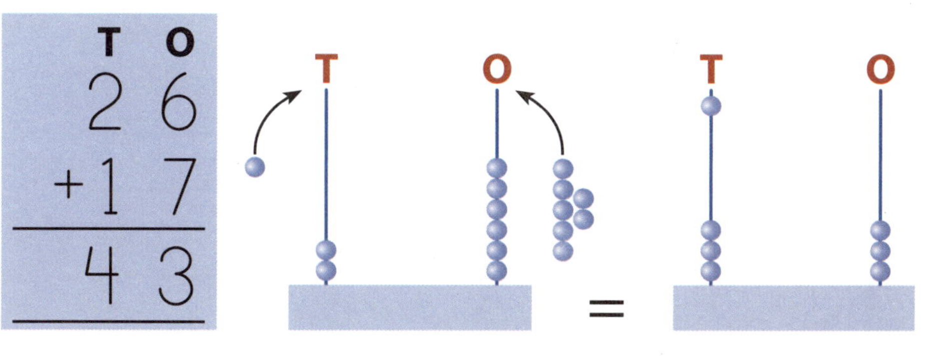

The ones stick should have 13, 3 remains 1 goes to 'T' stick.

This can also be explained by the following method.

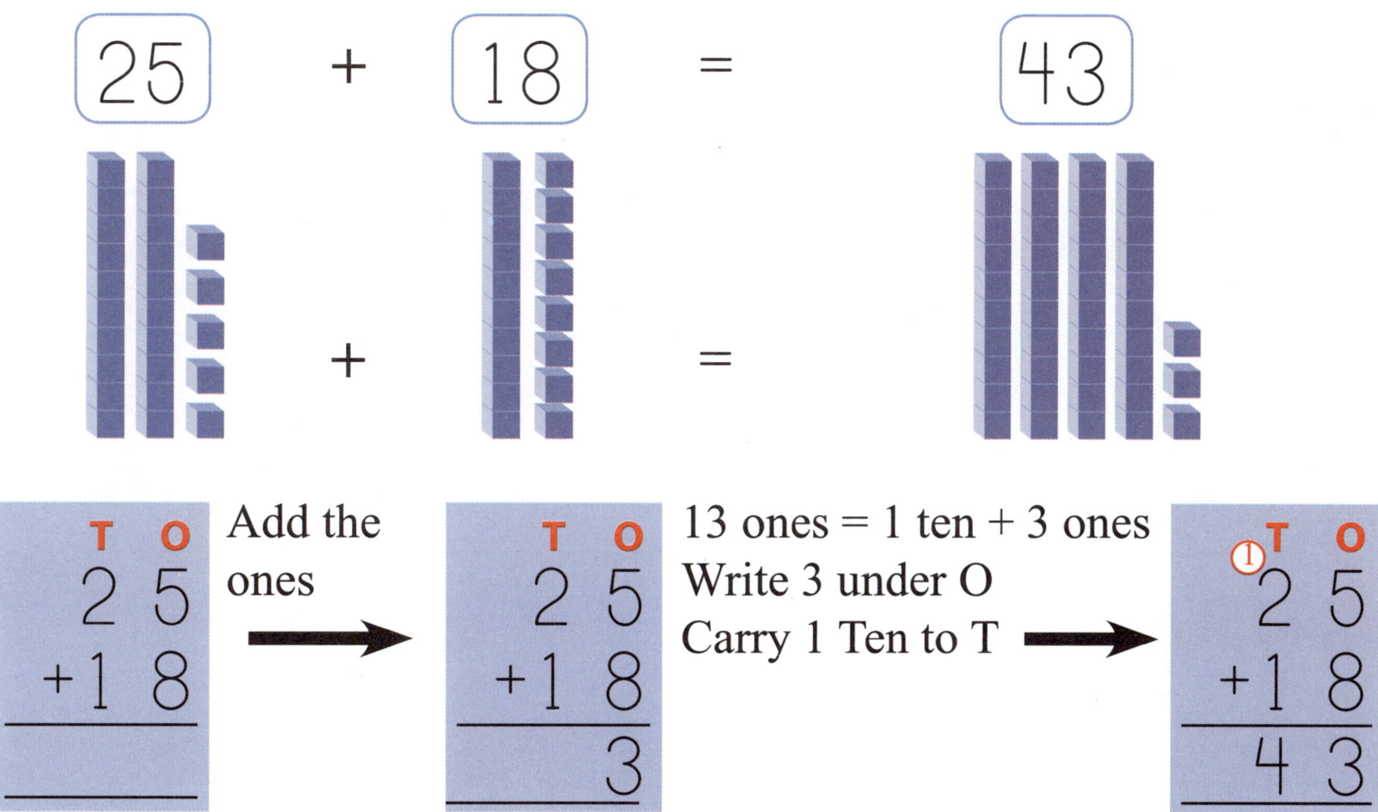

Write the digit to be 'carried over' here.

Practice to add

	T	O
	8	8
+		9

	T	O
	7	2
+	1	9

	T	O
	3	4
+	2	7

	T	O
	2	8
+	6	7

	T	O
	6	9
+	2	9

	T	O
	5	4
+	2	8

	T	O
	7	8
+		9

	T	O
	3	6
+	4	5

	T	O
	3	8
+	4	6

	T	O
	4	9
+	3	9

	T	O
	3	8
+	3	9

	T	O
	6	5
+	2	5

	T	O
	5	6
+	1	6

	T	O
	2	5
+	5	8

	T	O
	5	6
+	3	6

	T	O
	4	5
+	4	5

	T	O
	4	6
+	3	6

	T	O
	5	2
+	2	8

	T	O
	6	3
+	2	7

	T	O
	3	5
+	4	8

Word Problems (Addition)

In a toy shop, there are 39 cars and 56 trucks. How many toys in all?

Cars		39
Truck	+	56
Toys		

45 girls and 35 boys went on a picnic. How many students went in all?

Girls		
Boys	+	
Students		

There are 54 mangoes in a basket. 28 more mangoes are put into the basket. How many mangoes are there?

	+	
Mangoes		

There were 32 children on a school bus. 38 more got in. How many students were there in the bus?

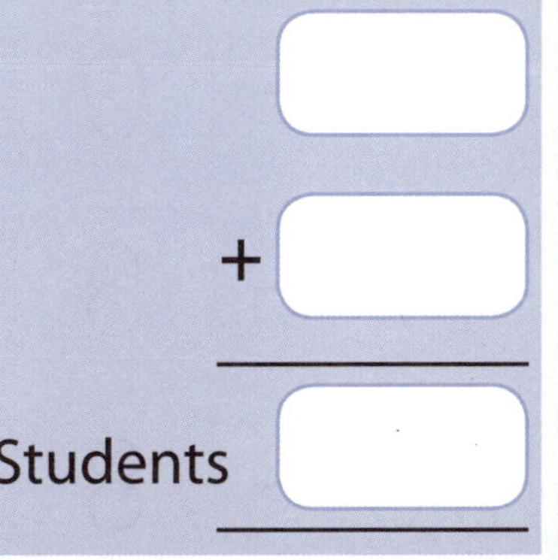

	+	
Students		

Subtraction

4

Let's Recall the Number Line.

Subtract- 8 – 5

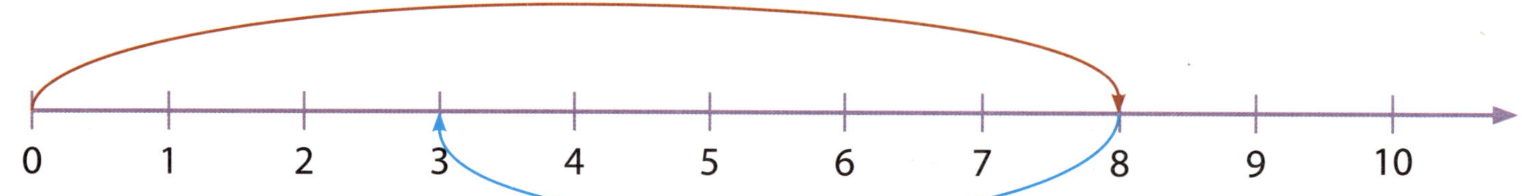

8 – 5 = 3

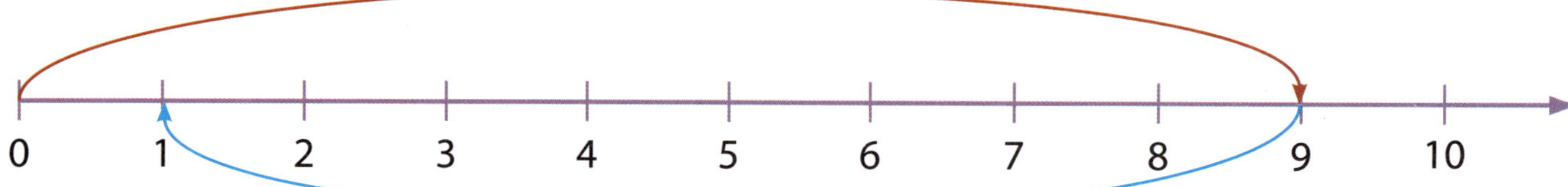

9 – 8 = 1

Subtract

9 – 9 = 0

9 – 0 =

17 – 3 = 14

20 – 8 =

19 – 5 =

18 – 6 = 12

20 – 6 =

17 – 4 =

Lab Activity

Teacher should encourage students to use abacus or paper strips or bundles of ice cream sticks (with loose sticks) to do the subtraction.

T O	T O	T O	T O	T O
36	88	39	43	56
−21	−66	−27	−21	−25
___	___	___	___	___

T O	T O	T O	T O	T O
98	65	83	27	91
−36	−22	−41	−15	−50
___	___	___	___	___

T O	T O	T O	T O	T O
75	85	66	33	22
−34	−84	−55	−20	−11
___	___	___	___	___

T O	T O	T O	T O	T O
44	65	99	97	89
−22	−35	−88	−66	−30
___	___	___	___	___

Subtraction with Borrowing

36 = 3 tens 6 ones

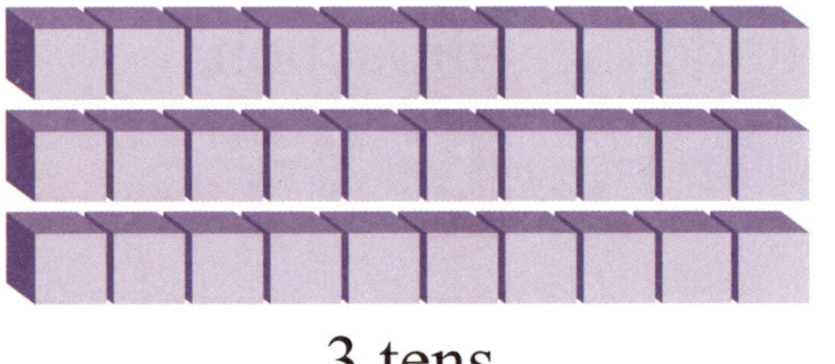

3 tens

+

6 ones

Regroup

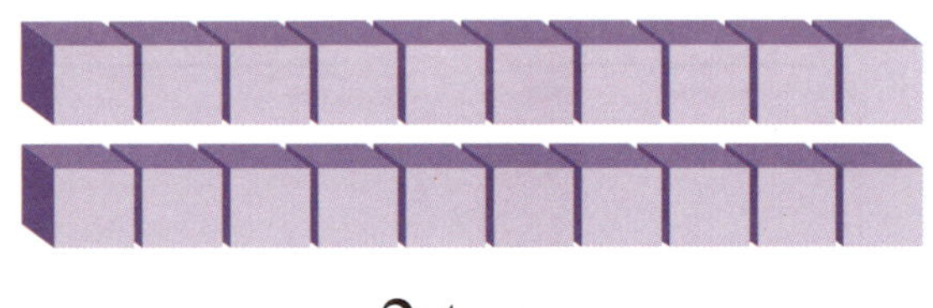

2 tens

+

16 ones

Regroup

24 = 2 tens 4 ones to

1 tens

+

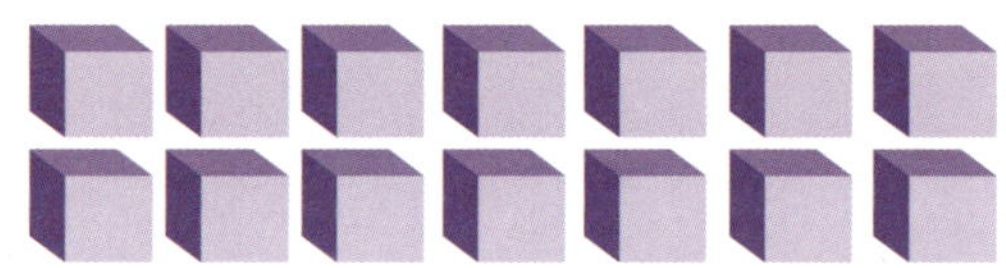

14 ones

We use regrouping for subtraction.

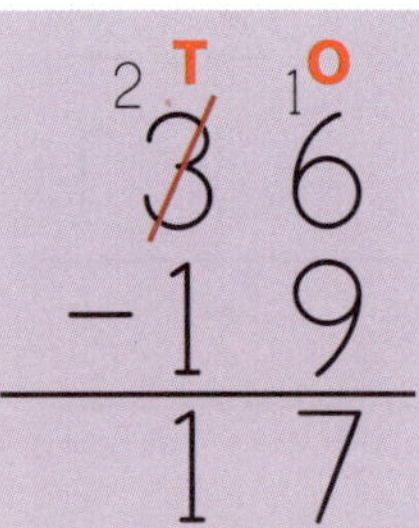

6 – 9 is not possible
But 16 – 9 is possible.
So, 1 is borrowed by 6 from 3 tens; it becomes 16 ones
16 – 9 = 7
3 tens becomes 2 tens
2 tens – 1 ten = 1 ten

Let us try for 68–39

T	O
5 ~~6~~	1 8
–3	9
2	9

8 becomes 18 by borrowing 1 from 6 tens.

6 tens becomes 5 tens.

Hence 18 – 9 = 9

and 5 – 3 = 2

Subtract: (Activity: Use a strip of paper for solving the sums.)

T O	T O	T O	T O
7 6 -3 9	4 5 -1 8	3 4 -2 7	9 0 -1 6
8 2 -5 8	6 3 -2 9	7 1 -3 5	5 2 -4 9
6 3 -2 7	4 2 -2 6	5 0 -2 5	7 3 -5 4
5 2 -2 5	7 4 -4 7	6 8 -4 9	7 4 -3 8
6 2 -3 5	6 1 -4 9	8 3 -7 4	6 3 -3 6

Subtract the following and borrow wherever required.

T O	T O	T O	T O
3 7 -1 6	7 4 -3 9	5 7 -2 9	4 2 -1 8
7 2 -5 8	5 4 -3 9	3 4 -1 9	6 1 -1 8
8 5 -6 9	6 8 -5 9	4 5 -2 9	5 7 -2 8
4 1 -3 7	6 8 -1 9	7 4 -6 6	8 0 -3 5
8 6 -7 9	9 0 - 8	7 7 -6 8	4 4 -2 8

Word Problems (Subtraction)

Out of 40 students in a class, 33 went on a picnic. How many did not go?

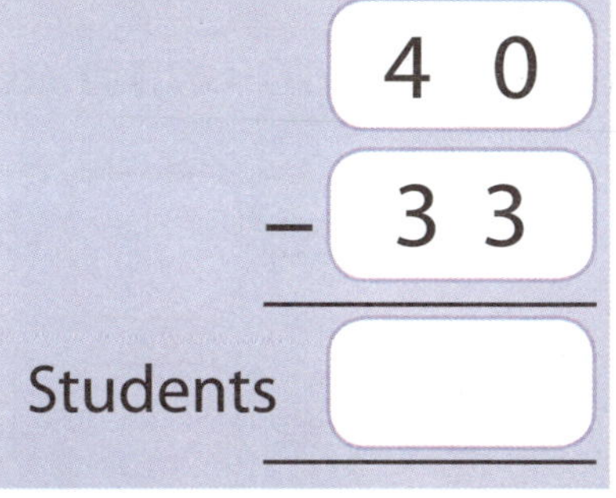

The story book has 92 pages. Mitchelle read 35 pages on the first day. How many pages are left?

Arthur brought 45 chocolates to give his friends on his birthday. He went home with 9 chocolates. How many did he distribute?

A box can hold 84 balls. 59 have been put inside. How many more balls can be put inside so that it is fully packed?

REVIEW EXERCISE 1

1. Write in expanded form.

76 = ☐ + ☐ 40 = ☐ + ☐

24 = ☐ + ☐ 39 = ☐ + ☐

2. Write number in the box.

3. Circle what comes before.

Thirty nine	40	38	41	50
Seventy	71	69	61	72

4. Write in descending order.

38 83 33 88

5. Write the place value of underlined digit in the box.

$\underline{6}4$ ☐ $9\underline{2}$ ☐ $\underline{5}0$ ☐ $\underline{7}5$ ☐

6. Add

T O
1 3
+2 0
+4 6

T O
5 8
+ 7

T O
3 5
+4 9

T O
+7 8
+2 2

7. Subtract

T O
5 7
− 8

T O
9 4
−3 6

T O
8 0
−6 8

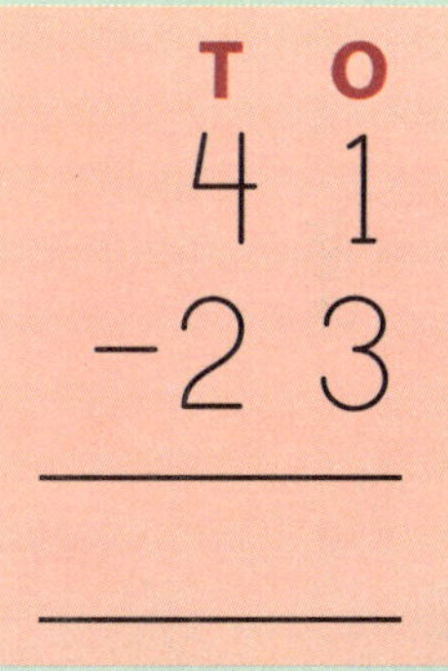

T O
4 1
−2 3

8. Out of 70 chairs, 24 are broken. How many chairs are in good condition?

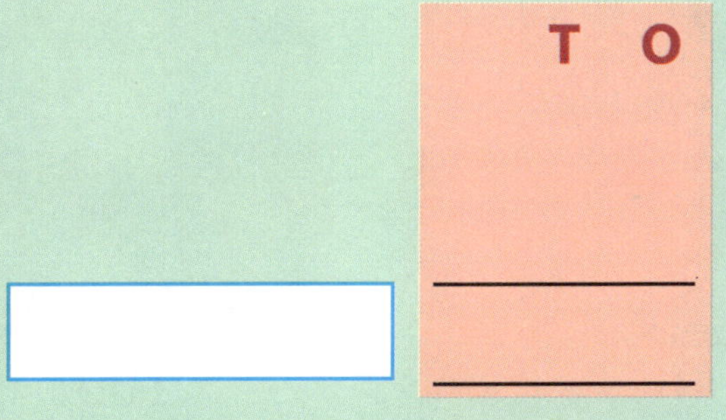

9. Along one side of a road there are 64 houses and on the other side, there are 58 houses. How many houses are there along the road?

Numbers from 101 to 200

5

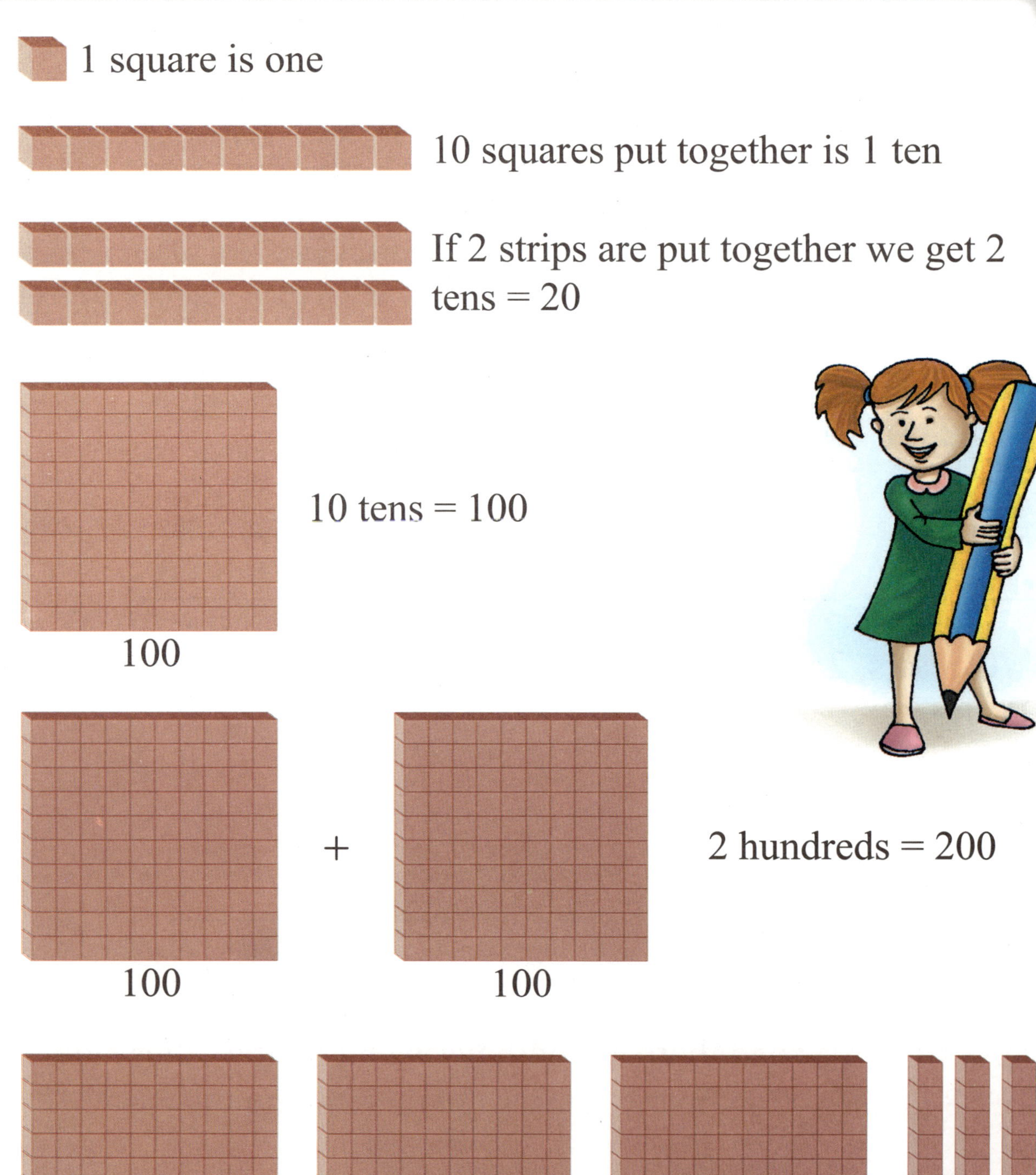

HTO
300 + 40 + 6 = 346

100

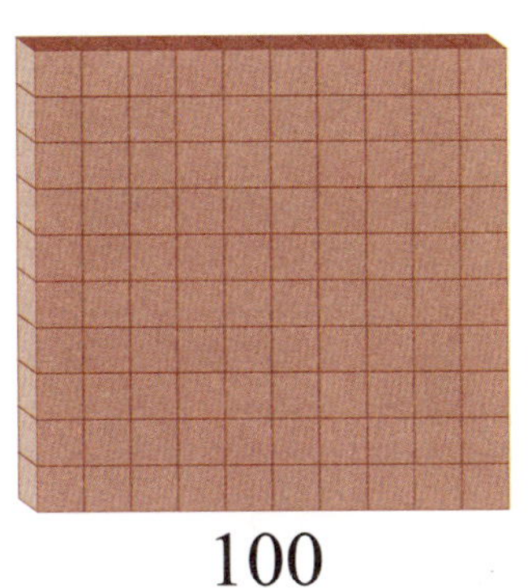

100 (a square grid with 100 small divisions)

100
+
10 10 10 10

= 100 + 40 = 140

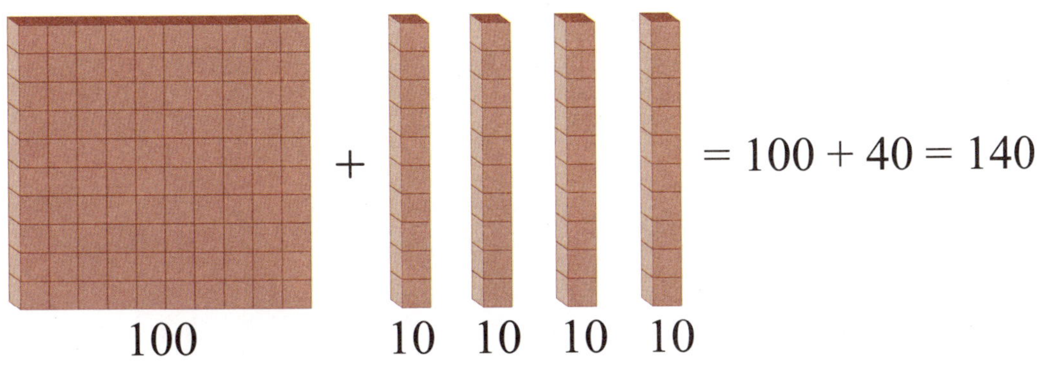

100 100 100
10 10 10
+
100 100 100
10 10 10

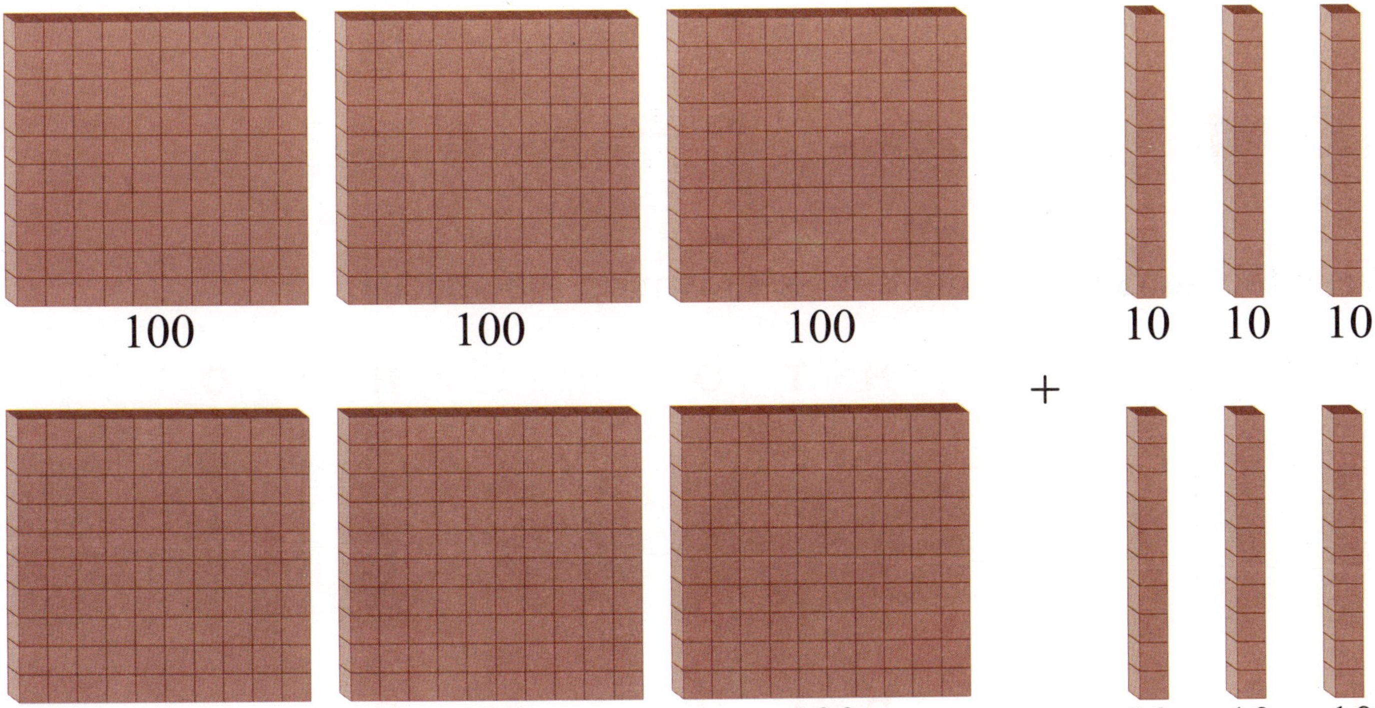

= 600 + 60

= 660

We can show these 3-digit numbers on an abacus also. We introduce the 3rd stick for the **hundreds place** now.

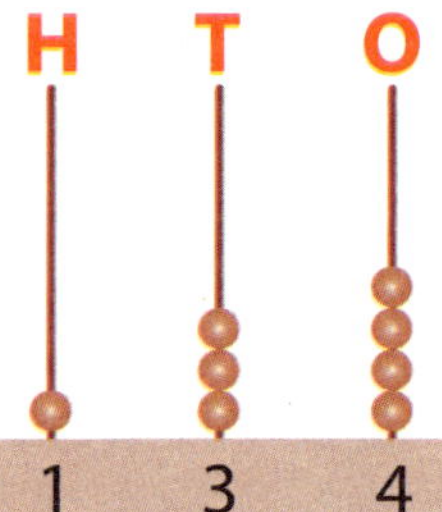

The number is 134

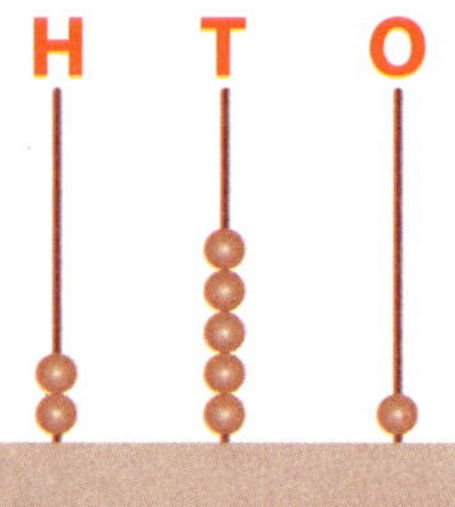

251 = 2 hundreds + 5 tens + 1 ones

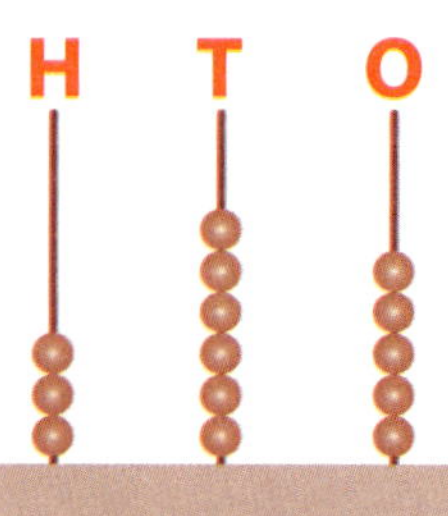

365 = 3 hundreds + 6 tens + 5 ones

Write the numerals in the box as shown on the abacus.

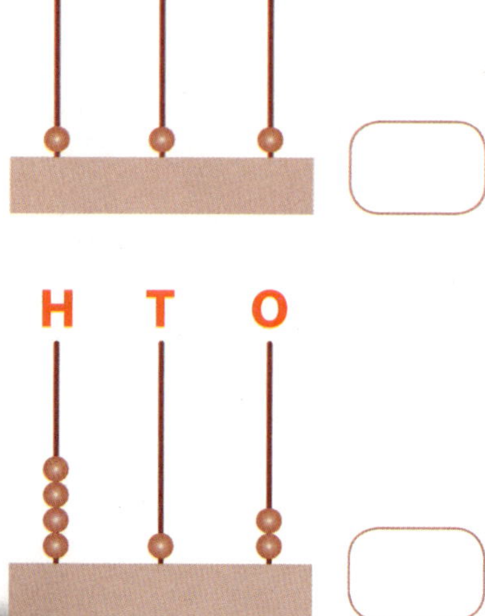

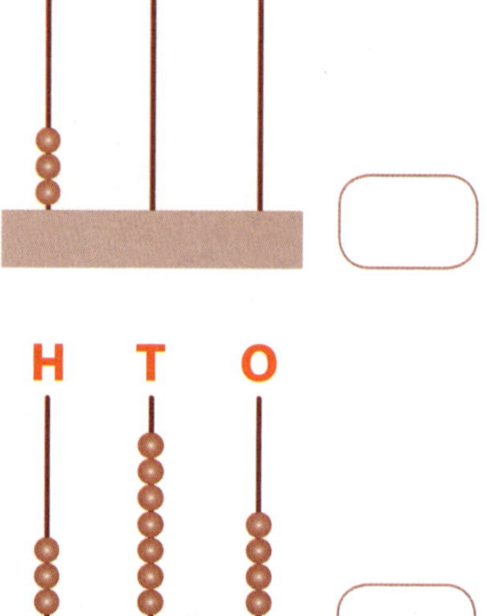

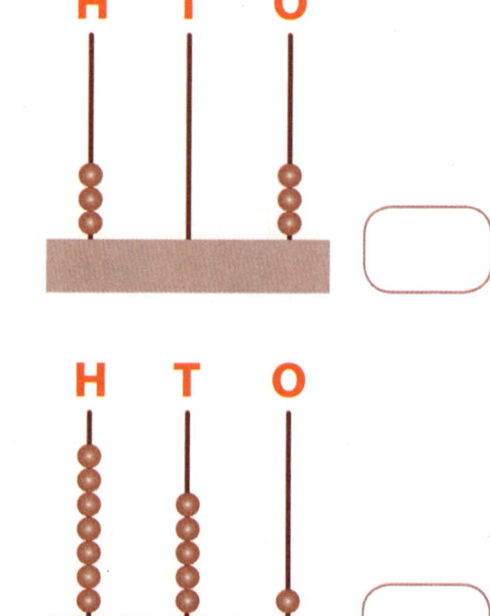

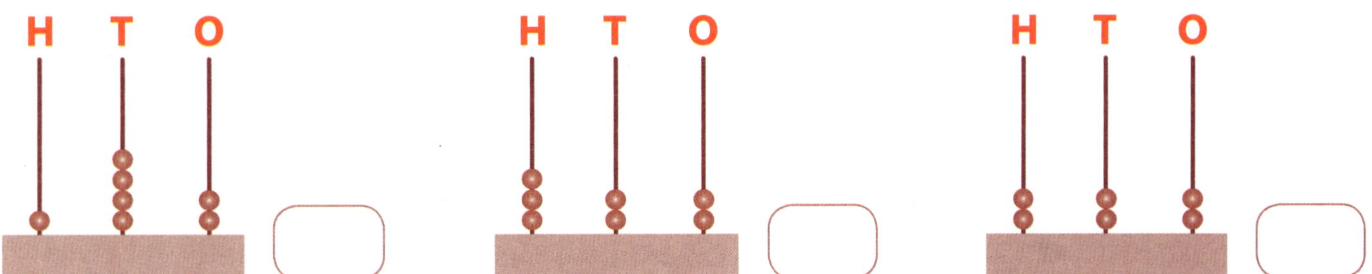

Put the beads in the abacus to show the numbers in the box.

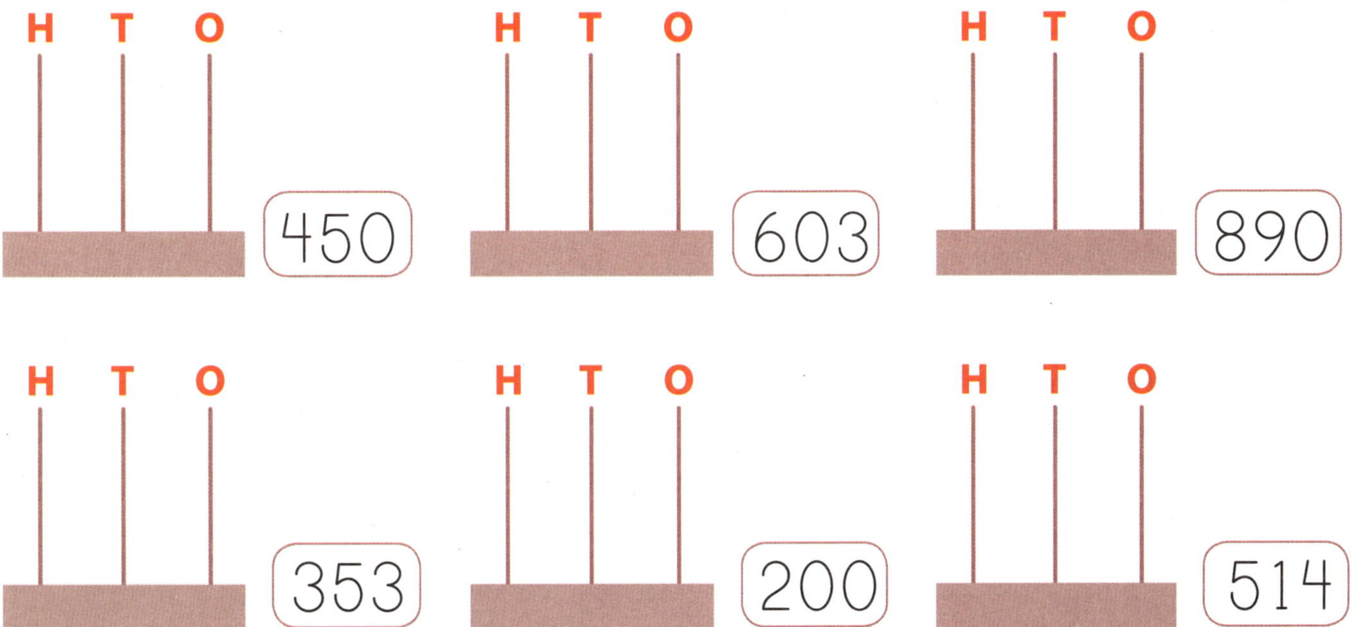

Place Value (3-digit numbers)

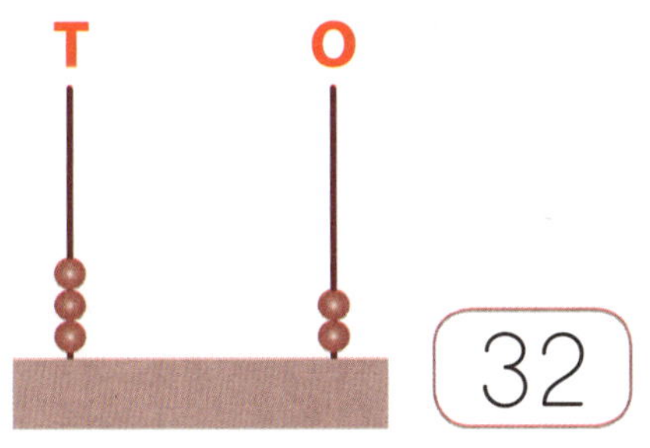

In 32, it is 3 tens or 30 and 2 ones or 2

In 32, 2 is in **ones place** and its value is 2.

In 25, it is 2 tens or 20 and 5 ones or 5

In 25, 2 is in **tens place** and its value is 20.

Let us see in 215

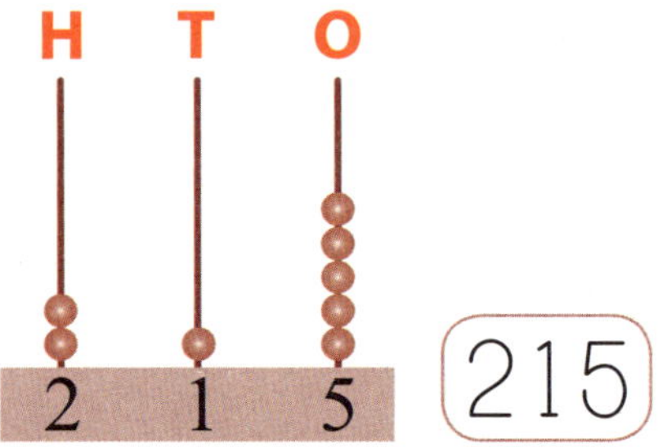

2 is in **hundreds place** and its value is 200.

The position of a digit changes its value.

Let us see in 316.

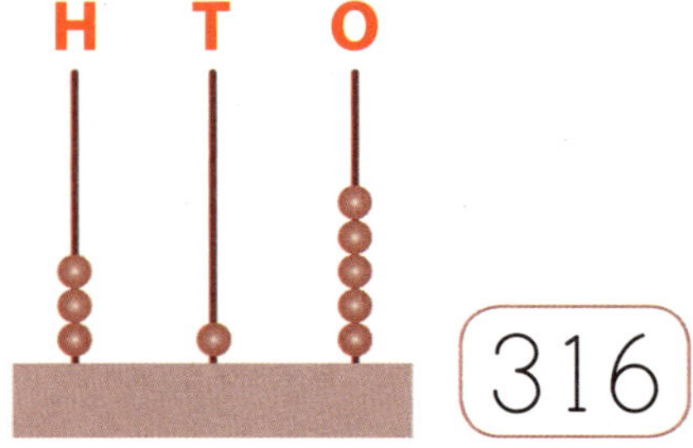

3 is in hundreds place; so, place value of 3 is 3 hundreds or 300. Place value of 1 is 1 ten or 10, place value of 6 is 6 ones or 6.

We need not draw the abacus every time. For example, in 478, write O, T and H above the digits.

HTO
478

Place value of 7 is 7 tens or 70.

Write the place value in the boxes.

2	in	128	is	20		9	in	942	is	
5	in	560	is			1	in	715	is	
3	in	143	is			7	in	172	is	
6	in	276	is			4	in	348	is	
0	in	109	is			2	in	200	is	
1	in	136	is			9	in	195	is	
5	in	754	is			3	in	302	is	
6	in	620	is			2	in	452	is	

See the place value of each digit and then arrange to make 3-digit numbers.

O	H	T	Number
4	3	6	364
9	6	9	
5	6	0	
2	4	0	
3	5	8	
6	4	5	
1	0	7	
0	8	4	
2	7	6	
3	2	4	

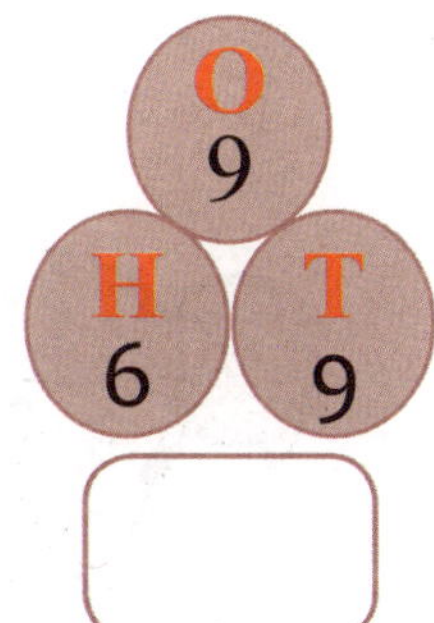

Write down the numeral for each sum.

200 + 70 + 3 = 273	300 + 60 + 8 =
800 + 50 + 9 =	800 + 30 + 4 =
600 + 60 + 6 =	200 + 0 + 5 =
100 + 50 + 0 =	700 + 10 + 0 =
400 + 0 + 5 =	500 + 10 + 9 =
700 + 20 + 3 =	900 + 70 + 1 =
500 + 40 + 4 =	400 + 30 + 3 =

Write in the expanded form.

645 = 600 + 40 + 5

930 = + +

471 = + +

384 = + +

182 = + +

600 = + +

835 = + +

3-Digit Numbers 101 - 200

What comes after 98?

98 + 1 = 99

After 99?   99 + 1 = 100

After 100?   100 + 1 = 101

Similarly,101 + 1 = 102 and so on.....

Now let us learn to write numbers from 101 to 200

Complete the given grid by counting forward:

101	102								110
111									
	122						128		
131					136				
		143						149	
				155					
					166				170
171			174						
	182					187			190
		193			196			199	

Now let us learn to write from 201 to 300

Complete the given grid

201					206				
	212								
					256				
261						267			
							278		
									290
									300

Now let us learn to write from 301 to 400

Complete the given grid

301									310
								319	
							328		
						337			
					346				
				255					
			364						
		373							
	382								
391									400

Now let us learn to write from 401 to 500

Complete the given grid

401									
					426				
				435		437		439	
			444				448		
				455		457			
					466				470
		483							
									500

Write number names

314	three hundred fourteen
438	
290	
117	

To write a 3-digit number first write the hundreds place then tens and ones place digits together

Write the numeral for the following.

Four hundred ninety nine ☐

Three hundred twenty ☐

Two hundred and four ☐

One hundred sixty ☐

Now let us learn to write from 501 to 600

Complete the given grid

501									510
						527			
	532								
				555					
							578		
591								599	

Now let us learn to write from 601 to 700

Complete the given grid

601									
						637			
					666				
		683							
									700

Now let us learn to write from 701 to 800

Complete the given grid

701									710
				725				729	
						737			
		743							
					756				
	772					777			
			784						
791				795					800

Now let us learn to write from 801 to 900

Complete the given grid

801									
	822								
						837			
		853							
						867			
	882						888		
891								899	

Fill in the missing numbers from 901-999

Complete the given grid

901									910
				955					
								969	
981									
								999	1000

Write the following numbers as indicated.

H T O

1. One more than 700 ______
2. One less than 510 ______
3. Ten more than 836 ______
4. Ten less than 675 ______
5. Five more than 549 ______

1000 comes after 999, it is the smallest 4-digit number

Show on Abacus

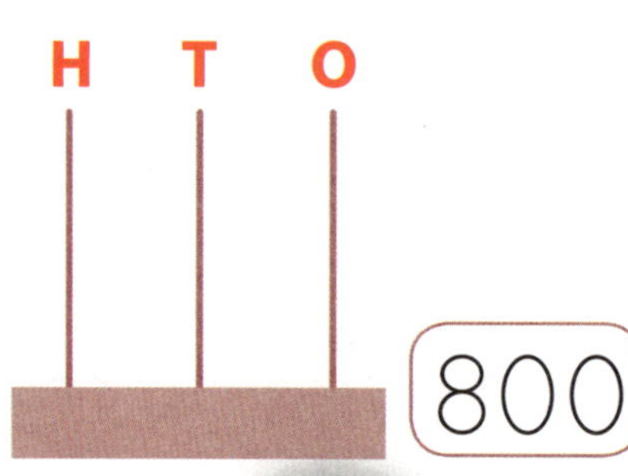

What comes before and after?

Before	Number	After
	400	
	650	
	731	
	879	

Before	Number	After
	675	
	488	
	599	
	964	

Read the number of beads on the abacus and fill the boxes with the numbers.

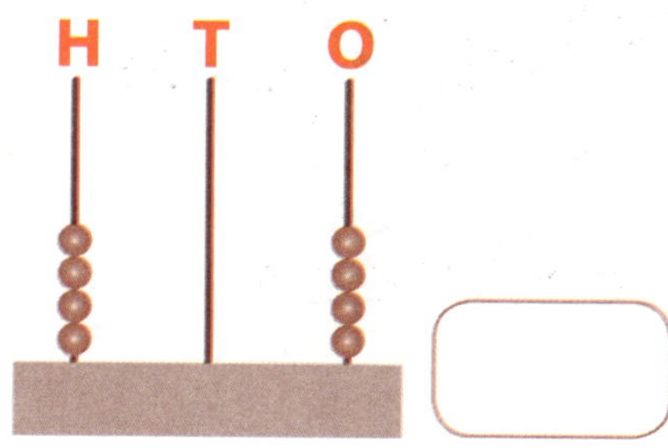

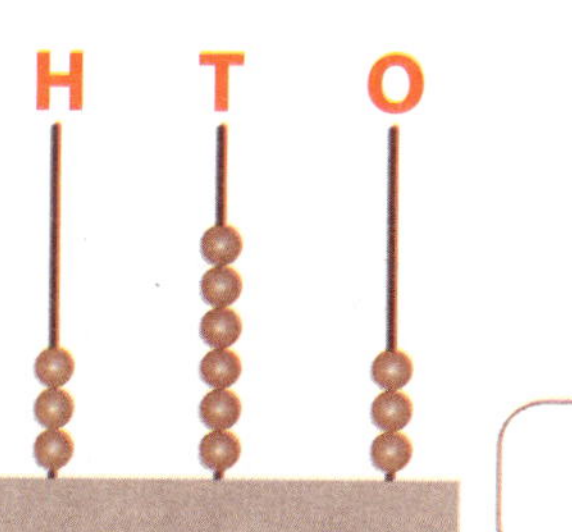

Write the numeral in the box.

3 hundred + 2 tens + 5 ones — 325

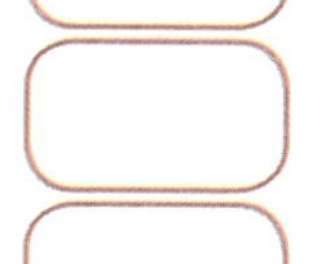

7 hundred + 7 ones

6 hundred + 8 tens

9 hundred + 9 tens + 9 ones

4 hundred 6 tens + 7 ones

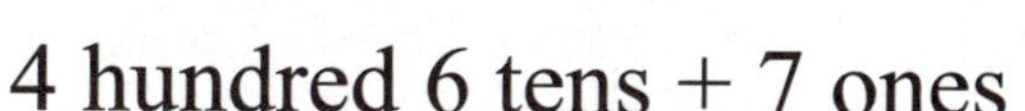

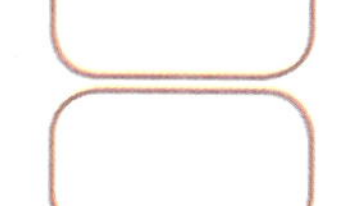

Write in the expanded form.

199 — 100 + 90 + 9

350

708

884

Comparing 3-Digit Numbers

1. Let us compare 3-digit numbers

372 and 298

Write HTO on the digits of each number like this

H	T	O
3	7	2

H	T	O
2	9	8

3 hundreds > 2 hundreds. So 372 > 298

2. Compare 263 and 248

H	T	O
2	4	8

H	T	O
2	6	3

Both have same digit in the hundreds place.

Compare the digits in the tens places.

6 tens > 4 tens. So 248 < 263

3. Compare 426 and 428

H	T	O
4	2	6

H	T	O
4	2	8

Steps to follow

First step – compare hundreds place. If same, then Second step – compare digits in tens place. If same, then Third step – Compare digits in ones place.

Both have same digits in hundreds and tens places.

Compare 6 ones and 8 ones.

6 ones < 8 ones. So 426 < 428

Compare and write '>' or '<' in the circle.

148	◯	203	111	◯	222	166	◯	611
209	◯	902	636	◯	631	500	◯	501
681	◯	618	199	◯	169	900	◯	109
75	◯	107	115	◯	511	254	◯	221
305	◯	350	206	◯	205	99	◯	201
561	◯	156	189	◯	191	368	◯	87
432	◯	433	701	◯	900	411	◯	100

Underline the **smallest** and circle the **greatest** in the following groups.

234	201	241	211	254	266	284
176	167	761	716	754	164	132
550	450	650	950	425	564	925
310	801	88	910	885	654	254
555	222	333	777	666	999	111

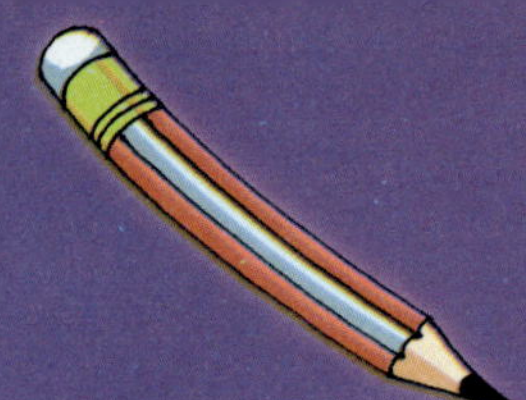

REVIEW EXERCISE 2

1. Fill in the boxes

   1. In 482, place value of 8 is ☐
   2. In 604, ☐ tens
   3. 500 + 80 + 4 = ☐
   4. 10 less than 730 is ☐

2. Write 3-digit numbers using the following digits.

   1. 4, 1, 3 – 134, 143, 341, 314, 413, 431
   2. 5, 6, 2 – ☐ ☐ ☐ ☐ ☐ ☐
   3. 0, 8, 9 – ☐ ☐ ☐ ☐ ☐ ☐

3. Who am I?

   I am a 2-digit number with 1 in the ones place. I am greater than 75 and smaller than 83. Who am I? ☐

4. Write the number name for

   1. 350 – ....
   2. 728 – ....

5. Write the numeral.

   1. One hundred and ten – ....
   2. Six hundred – ....

Addition of 3-Digit Numbers

6

Study the following addition sums

Add 342 and 215

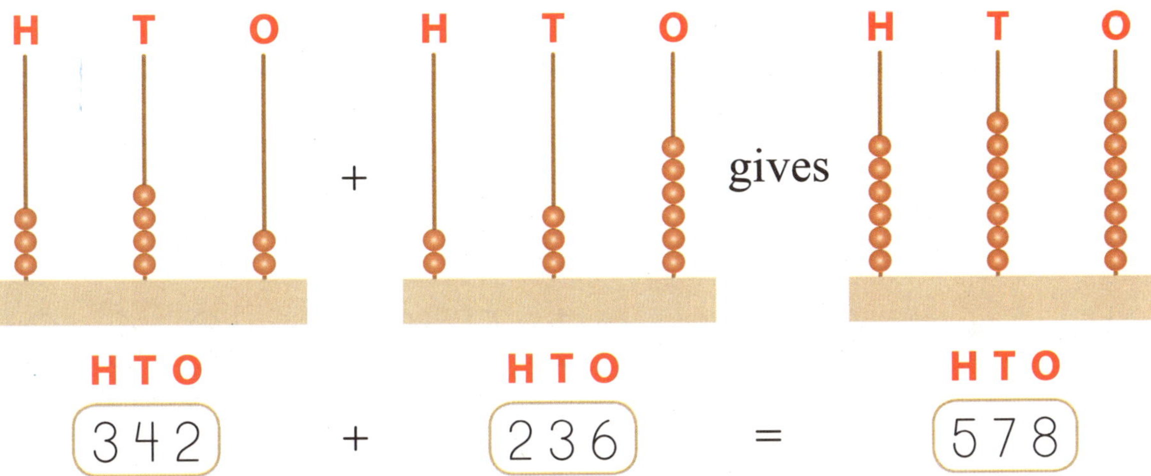

	H	T	O
	3	4	2
+	2	3	6
	5	7	8

First add the digits in ones place, then digits in tens place are added, and finally the digits in hundred's place are added.

Add and fill in the boxes

	H	T	O
	1	2	6
+	2	3	1

	H	T	O
	3	4	1
+	2	0	8

	H	T	O
	4	0	7
+	3	5	0

	H	T	O
	3	2	1
+	1	7	8

Add and fill in the boxes

H	T	O
5	0	6
+3	0	0

H	T	O
7	1	6
+2	8	3

H	T	O
3	2	9
+4	0	0

H	T	O
3	7	0
+2	2	2

H	T	O
6	0	4
+2	8	4

H	T	O
5	5	5
+4	0	4

H	T	O
6	0	8
+1	8	0

H	T	O
3	1	7
+2	6	0

H	T	O
1	2	3
+4	5	6
+2	1	0

H	T	O
1	4	7
+2	5	1
+1	0	0

H	T	O
6	5	4
+	2	3
+	1	1

H	T	O
3	3	3
+	6	5
+		1

H	T	O
7	3	3
+1	2	2
+	4	4

H	T	O
1	5	3
+2	2	1
+		5

H	T	O
3	3	5
+3	4	0
+	2	9

H	T	O
5	2	1
+1	2	5
+	3	3

Addition of 3-Digits Numbers with Carrying

Add 427 and 356

Use an abacus

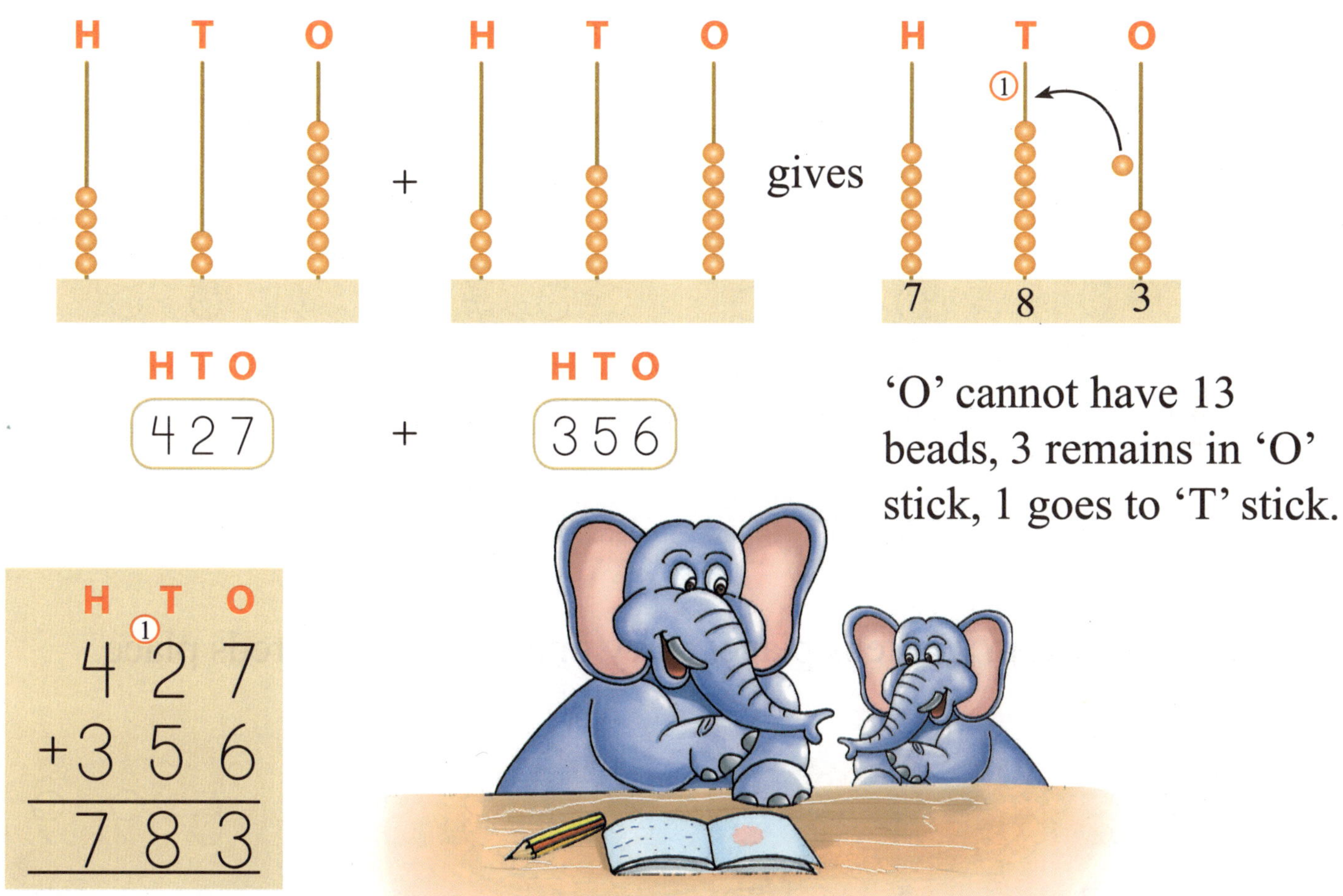

Lab Activity

Students can use abacus or number strips for the addition.

H T O	H T O	H T O	H T O
5 6 9	7 3 4	2 4 5	8 0 8
+3 1 3	+1 1 6	+1 0 7	+1 4 7

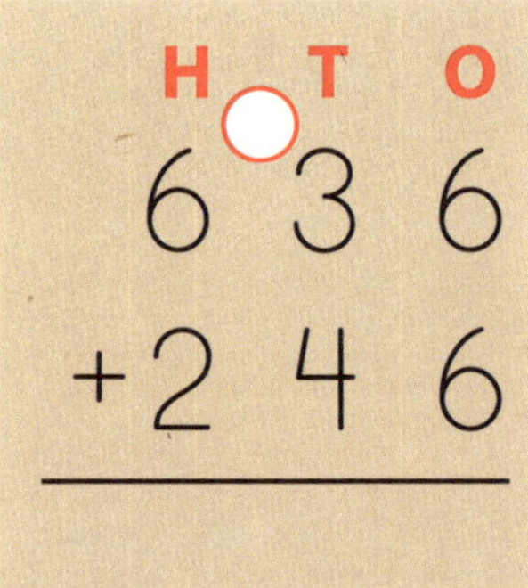

H T O: 3 3 1 + 4 0 9

H T O: 4 6 6 + 3 6

H T O: 4 3 9 + 1 0 2

H T O: 5 5 5 + 1 1 7

H T O: 6 0 6 + 3 0 8

H T O: 5 7 8 + 2 1 3

H T O: 8 8 9 + 1 0 1

If there is more than 9 in tens place, carry one over to hundreds place.

H T O: (1)(1) 3 3 3 + 4 7 7 = 8 1 0

H T O: 4 6 5 + 1 6 5

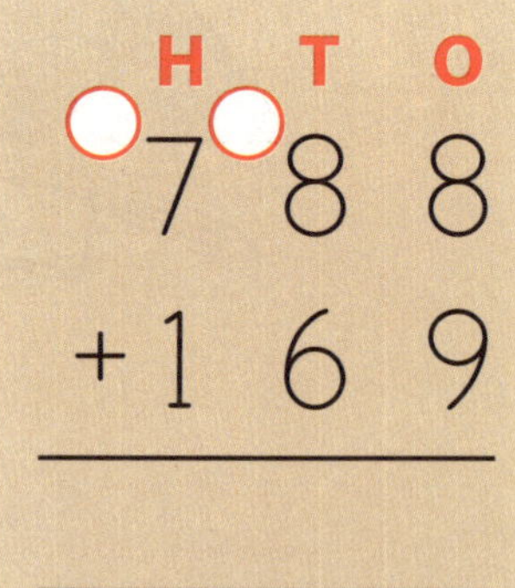

H T O: 5 9 9 + 1 5 2

H T O: 5 9 4 + 1 7 7

H T O: 2 9 3 + 1 1 8

H T O: 3 7 5 + 2 2 5

H T O: 7 0 3 + 2 2 2

Add (Remember : first add 'ones', next 'tens' and finally 'hundreds')

H	T	O
2	5	6
+3	6	5
+	5	3

H	T	O
5	8	3
+2	1	7
+1	3	4

H	T	O
4	3	7
+2	8	6
+2	5	4

H	T	O
6	2	8
+1	8	7
+	3	4

H	T	O
7	5	9
+1	6	7

H	T	O
4	9	6
+2	1	5

H	T	O
3	7	8
+1	3	8

H	T	O
6	4	8
+2	6	3

H	T	O
5	6	5
+1	9	9

H	T	O
3	3	8
+2	7	4

H	T	O
1	4	6
+2	8	0

H	T	O
1	7	3
+1	8	0

H	T	O
3	5	7
+2	7	6

H	T	O
4	8	9
+2	3	1

H	T	O
1	7	1
+3	8	9

H	T	O
2	0	6
+1	9	6

Word Problems (On Addition)

A library has 318 books. 230 more books were bought. How many books does the library have now?

	318
+	230
Books	

In a school there are 535 boys and 375 girls. How many students are there in the school?

Boys	
Girls	
Students	

In a fruit stall, 458 mangoes, 326 bananas and 65 apples are there. How many fruits are there in the stall?

Mangoes	
Bananas	
Apples	
Fruits	

It takes 275 days to build a mall and 188 days to paint it. How many days did it take to complete the mall?

Days to build	
Days to paint	
Days	

Subtraction of 3-Digit Numbers

7

Subtract 457-324

H	T	O
4	5	7
-3	2	4
1	3	3

Step 1: Subtract ones

Step 2: Subtract tens

Step 3: Subtract hundreds.

(Teacher should encourage students to use number line or abacus to subtract, till they start doing it **mentally**.)

Subtract and fill in the boxes.

H	T	O
5	8	5
-3	4	5

H	T	O
9	4	8
-2	3	1

H	T	O
6	8	0
-5	3	0

H	T	O
4	2	4
-2	1	2

H	T	O
8	8	8
-6	6	6

H	T	O
5	9	5
-5	8	1

H	T	O
6	1	4
-6	1	3

H	T	O
7	3	8
-5	1	6

Subtraction with Borrowing

Subtract

```
 H  T  O
    4  1
 2  5̸  6
-1  3  8
---------
       8
```

We cannot subtract 8 ones from 6 ones. So, borrow one 1 from 5 tens. We have 16 ones. 16 ones – 8 ones = 8 ones.

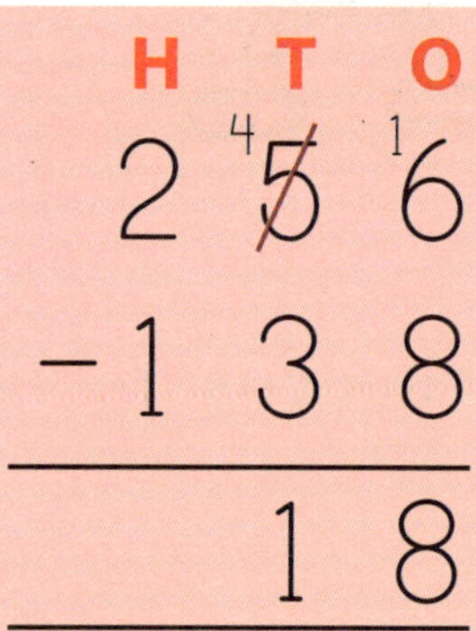

We have 4 tens left

Now take away 3 tens from 4 tens. 1 ten is left

Now take away 1 hundred from 2 hundreds. 1 hundred is left

Subtract

H T O	H T O	H T O	H T O
3 6 8	7 5 0	8 7 1	7 3 2
-2 3 9	-1 2 4	-5 3 6	-2 4 5
____	____	____	____

H	T	O
3	3	5
-1	1	7

H	T	O
6	4	6
-3	3	8

H	T	O
5	2	3
-2	0	5

H	T	O
5	8	1
-5	4	0

H	T	O
3	4	0
-2	8	1

H	T	O
4	6	6
-2	7	9

H	T	O
7	6	2
-	3	4

H	T	O
7	3	4
-3	6	5

H	T	O
8	1	3
-2	3	8

H	T	O
9	2	0
-3	5	5

H	T	O
6	4	0
-5	8	8

H	T	O
4	6	1
-3	6	2

H	T	O
5	0	0
-2	2	3

H	T	O
4	3	4
-	6	5

H	T	O
6	0	0
-1	3	4

H	T	O
7	2	0
-4	3	9

Word Problems (On Subtraction)

In a cricket match England scored 300 runs. West Indies scored 138 less. How many runs did West Indies score?

England's score	3 0 0
Less runs –	1 3 8
West Indies' score	

In a fish tank there are 283 fishes. 95 died. How many are left in the tank?

Fish	
Dead fish	
Fishes left	

A library has 732 books. 289 books were torn. How many books were in good condition?

Books	
Torn Books	
Good books	

A train is carrying 450 passengers. 162 passengers get down in the first station. How many passengers are left on the train?

Passengers	
Get down	
Passengers left	

Multiplication

Adding equal groups

A bicycle has 2 wheels.

Two bicycles have 2 + 2 = 4 wheels.

Five bicycles will have 2 + 2 + 2 + 2 + 2 = 10 wheels.

Bunch of 5 cherries

Bunch of 5 cherries

There are 10 cherries in all

How many groups are there? 2

How many cherries in 1 group? ___

So, 2 groups of 5 = 10

5 + 5 = 10

4 + ___ + ___ = ___

3 groups of [ ] = [ ]

3 groups of 2 = 2 + 2 + 2 = 6

We also say 3 times 2 = 6

We write it as 3 × 2 = 6

10 + 10 = 20

2 times 10 = 20

2 × 10 = 20

5 + 5 + 5 + 5 = 20

4 × 5 = [ ]

[ ] + [ ] + [ ] = 3 × [ ] = [ ]

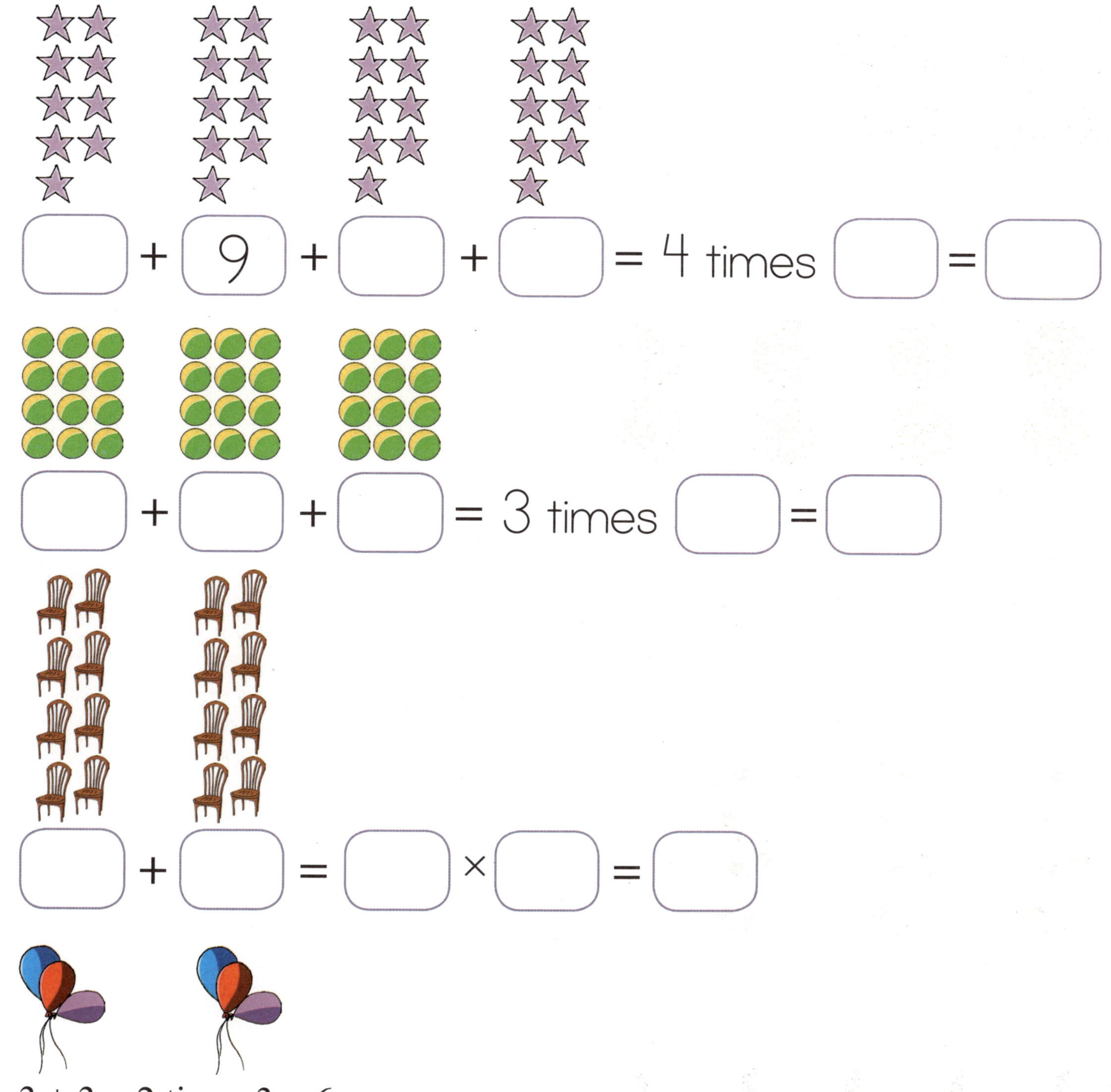

3 + 3 = 2 times 3 = 6

6 is the **product**.

2 times 3 can be written as 2 × 3.

'×' is the sign for multiplication.

Teacher should stress on '**product**' and should remind that when 2 or more numbers are added we get '**sum**' when 2 numbers are multiplied, we get ' **product**'.

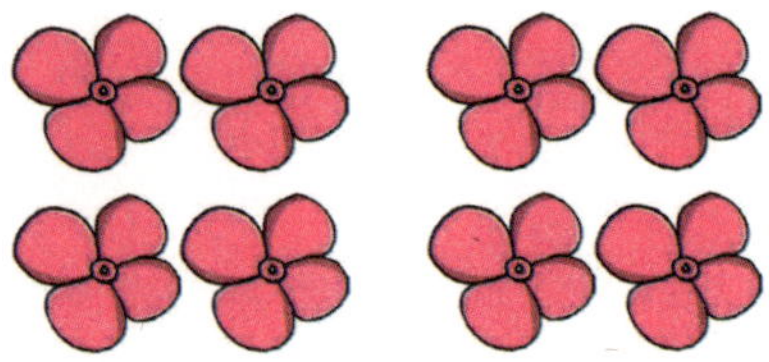

4 + 4 is 2 times 4 = 2 × 4 = 8

2 + 2 + 2 + 2 4 times 2 = 4 × 2 = 8

2 × 4 = 8 = 4 × 2

5 + 5 + 5 = 3 times 5 = 3 × 5 = 15

3 + 3 + 3 + 3 + 3 5 times 3 = 5 × 3 = 15

3 × 5 = 15 = 5 × 3

Fill in the boxes

3	×	5	=	5	×	3
3	×	4	=	4	×	
6	×	2	=		×	6
4	×	1	=	1	×	
5	×		=	7	×	

Use marbles or beads to find these.

4	×	2	=	2 + 2 + 2 + 2	=	8
6	×	1	=	1 + 1 + 1 + 1 + 1 + 1	=	6
2	×	7	=		=	
3	×	4	=		=	
2	×	5	=		=	
3	×	3	=		=	
8	×	2	=		=	

Multiplication on a Number Line

3 times 4

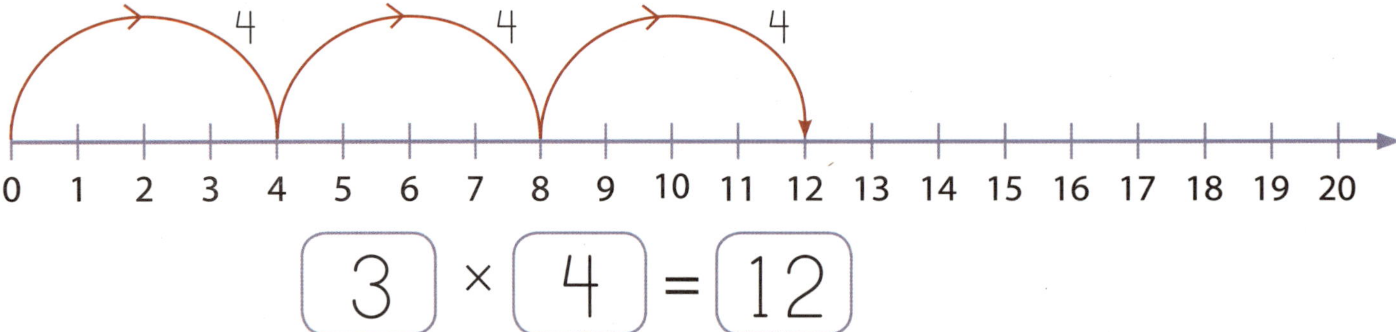

3 × 4 = 12

6 times 3

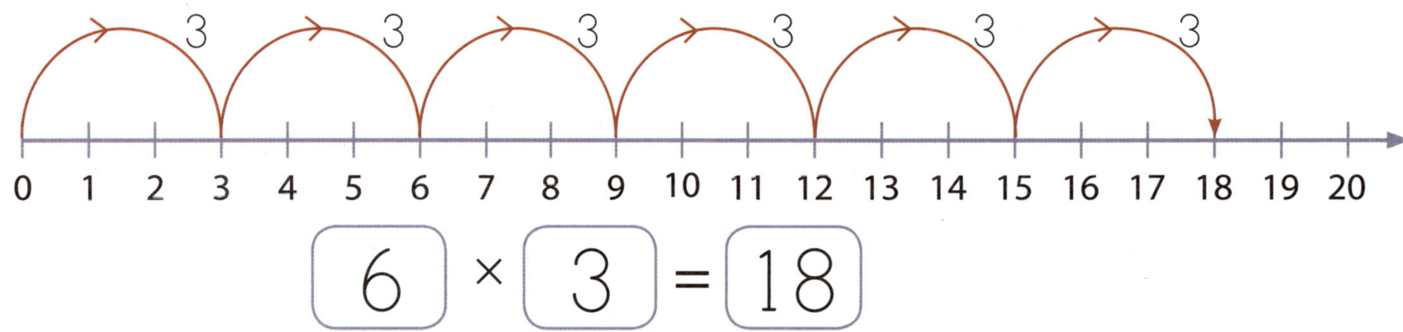

6 × 3 = 18

5 times 4

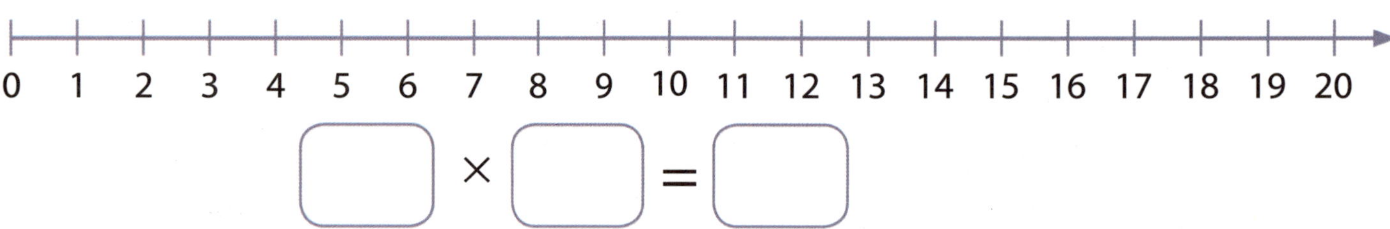

☐ × ☐ = ☐

3 times 7

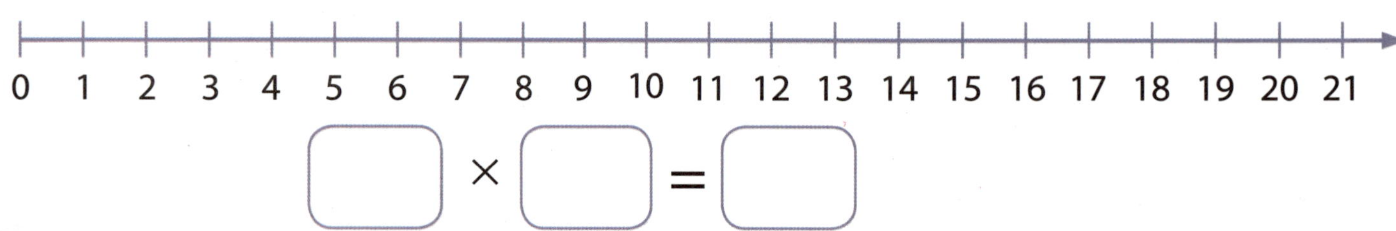

☐ × ☐ = ☐

How many times 2?

1 time 2 is [1] × [2] = [2]

2 times 2 is [2] × [2] = [4]

3 times 2 is [3] × [2] = [6]

4 times 2 is [ ] × [ ] = [ ]

5 times 2 is [ ] × [ ] = [ ]

6 times 2 is [ ] × [ ] = [ ]

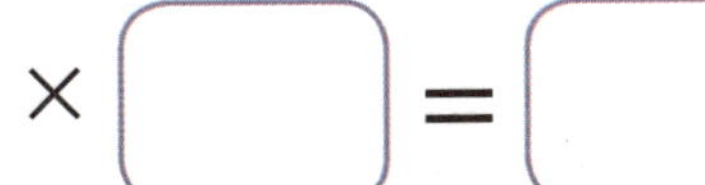

7 times 2 is [ ] × [ ] = [ ]

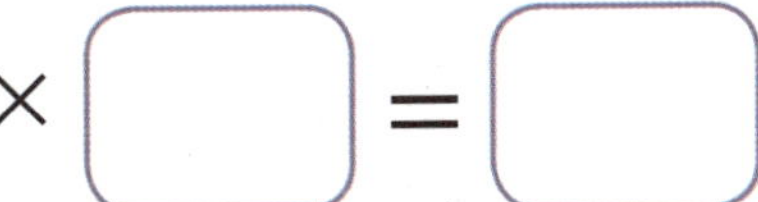

8 times 2 is [ ] × [ ] = [ ]

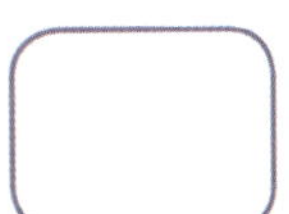

9 times 2 is [ ] × [ ] = [ ]

10 times 2 is [ ] × [2] = [20]

Multiplication Table of 3

Jump 3 steps at a time.

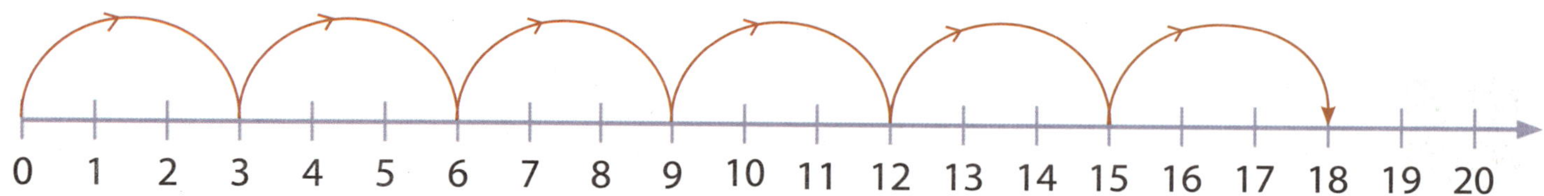

1 time 3 =	1	×	3	=	3
2 times 3 =	2	×	3	=	6
3 times 3 =		×		=	
4 times 3 =		×		=	
5 times 3 =		×		=	
6 times 3 =		×		=	
7 times 3 =		×		=	
8 times 3 =		×		=	
9 times 3 =		×		=	
10 times 3 =	10	×	3	=	30

Word Problems

There are 3 eggs in columns. There are 4 columns. How many eggs?

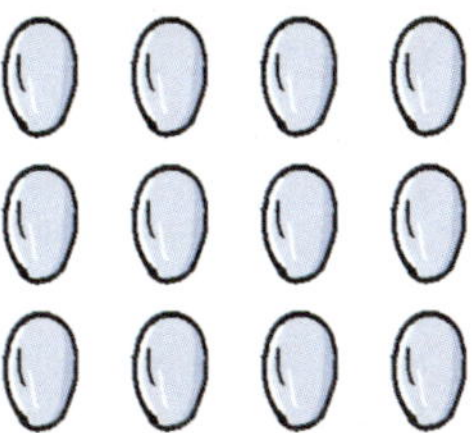

3 × 4 = 12

A bicycle has 2 wheels. There are 8 bicycles. What is the total number of wheels?

8 × 2 = ☐

Ms. Lisa gives 2 chocolates to her 9 students. How many chocolates did she give in all?

9 × 2 = ☐

Multiplication Table of 4

Jump 4 steps at a time.

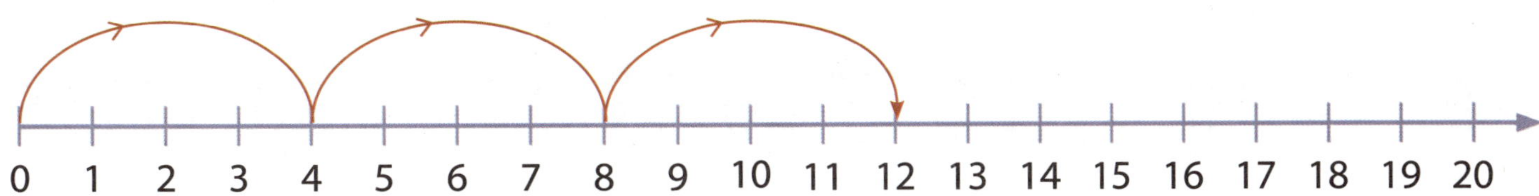

1 time 4 = 1 × 4 = 4

2 times 4 = 2 × 4 = 8

3 times 4 = ☐ × ☐ = ☐

4 times 4 =		×		=	
5 times 4 =		×		=	
6 times 4 =		×		=	
7 times 4 =		×		=	
8 times 4 =		×		=	
9 times 4 =		×		=	
10 times 4 =		×		=	

Multiplication Table of 5

Jump 5 steps at a time.

5 →+5 10 →+5 15 →+5 20 →+5 25 →+5 30 →+5 35 ↓+5 40 ←+5 45 ←+5 50

1 time 5 =	1	×	5	=	5
2 times 5 =	2	×	5	=	10
3 times 5 =		×		=	

4 times 5 = ☐ × ☐ = ☐

5 times 5 = ☐ × ☐ = ☐

6 times 5 = ☐ × ☐ = ☐

7 times 5 = ☐ × ☐ = ☐

8 times 5 = ☐ × ☐ = ☐

9 times 5 = ☐ × ☐ = ☐

10 times 5 = ☐ × ☐ = ☐

Multiplication Table of 6

Jump 6 steps at a time.

6 →+6 12 →+6 18 →+6 24 →+6 30 →+6 36 →+6 42 ↓+6 48 ←+6 54 ←+6 60

1 time 6 = 1 × 6 = 6

2 times 6 = 2 × 6 = 12

3 times 6 = ☐ × ☐ = ☐

4 times 6 = ☐ × ☐ = ☐

5 times 6 = ☐ × ☐ = ☐

6 times 6 = ☐ × ☐ = ☐

7 times 6 = ☐ × ☐ = ☐

8 times 6 = ☐ × ☐ = ☐

9 times 6 = ☐ × ☐ = ☐

10 times 6 = ☐ × ☐ = ☐

Word Problems

A shirt has 5 buttons. How many buttons would be there in 9 such shirts?

A flower has 6 petals. How many petals are there in 7 such flowers?

One necklace has 6 beads. How many beads are there in 10 such necklaces?

Multiplication table of 7

1 time 7 is	1	×	7	=	7
2 times 7 is		×		=	
3 times 7 is		×		=	
4 times 7 is		×		=	
5 times 7 is		×		=	
6 times 7 is		×		=	
7 times 7 is		×		=	
8 times 7 is		×		=	
9 times 7 is		×		=	
10 times 7 is		×		=	

Multiplication table of 8

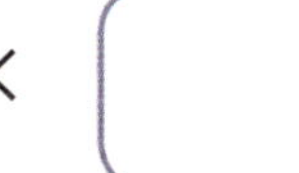

1 time 8 is	1	×	8	=	8
2 times 8 is		×		=	
3 times 8 is		×		=	

4 times 8 is ☐ × ☐ = ☐

5 times 8 is ☐ × ☐ = ☐

6 times 8 is ☐ × ☐ = ☐

7 times 8 is ☐ × ☐ = ☐

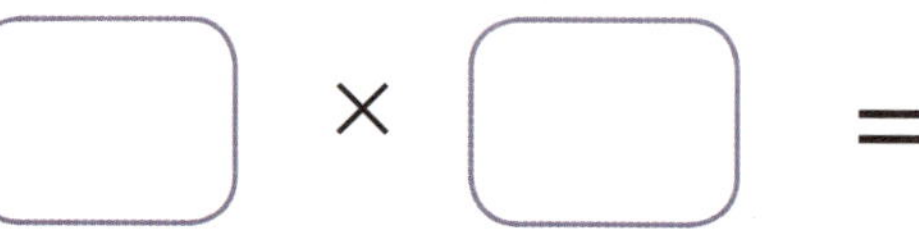

8 times 8 is ☐ × ☐ = ☐

9 times 8 is ☐ × ☐ = ☐

Multiplication table of 9

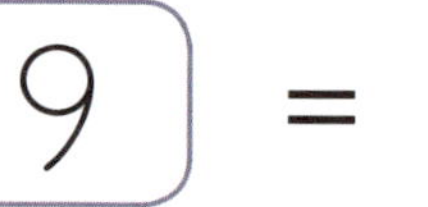

1 time 9 is 1 × 9 = 9

2 times 9 is ☐ × ☐ = ☐

3 times 9 is ☐ × ☐ = ☐

4 times 9 is ☐ × ☐ = ☐

5 times 9 is ☐ × ☐ = ☐

6 times 9 is ☐ × ☐ = ☐

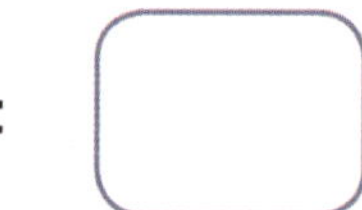

7 times 9 is ☐ × ☐ = ☐

8 times 9 is		×		=
9 times 9 is		×		=
10 times 9 is		×		=

Multiplication table of 10

1 time 10 is	1	×	10	=	10
2 times 10 is		×		=	
3 times 10 is		×		=	
4 times 10 is		×		=	
5 times 10 is		×		=	
6 times 10 is		×		=	
7 times 10 is		×		=	
8 times 10 is		×		=	
9 times 10 is		×		=	
10 times 10 is		×		=	

Word Problems

1 week has 7 days. How many days will be there in 9 weeks?

7 × 9 = ☐ Days

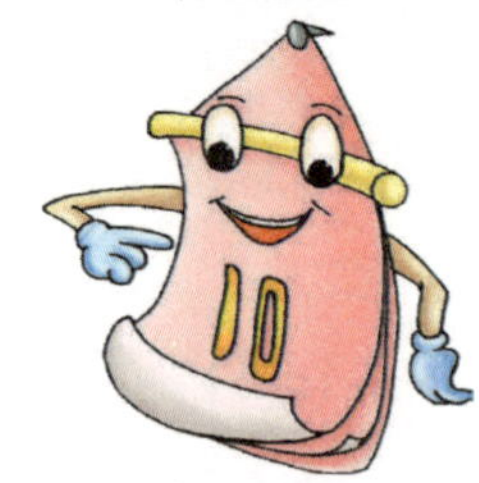

1 box has 10 crayons. How many crayons will be there in 10 boxes?

 ×  = ☐ Crayons

1 child is given 8 balloons. How many balloons will be needed for 8 children?

 × ☐ = ☐ Balloons

7 chairs are to be put in 1 row. How many chairs will be needed to put in 9 rows?

 ×  = ☐ Chairs

Multiplication by Zero

$0 + 0 + 0 = 0$

$0 + 0 + 0 + 0 + 0 + 0 = 0$

3 times $0 = 0 \times 3 = 0$

6 times $0 = 6 \times 0 = 0$

Any number $\times\ 0 = 0$

$0\ \times$ any number $= 0$

If you multiply any number by 0, the product is always 0. $5\times0=0$, $1\times0=0$

Exercise

Fill in the boxes

$4 \times 6 = \square$ | $5 \times 6 = \square$ | $6 \times 7 = \square$

$3 \times 8 = \square$ | $6 \times 0 = \square$ | $8 \times 4 = \square$

$2 \times 7 = \square$ | $9 \times 1 = \square$ | $9 \times 8 = \square$

$9 \times 2 = \square$ | $2 \times 10 = \square$ | $7 \times 8 = \square$

$6 \times 3 = \square$ | $4 \times 9 = \square$ | $10 \times 6 = \square$

$4 \times 10 = \square$ | $7 \times 5 = \square$ | $9 \times 6 = \square$

$8 \times 0 = \square$ | $6 \times 9 = \square$ | $5 \times 9 = \square$

Fill in the boxes given below

$6 \times \square = 30$ | $8 \times \square = 0$ | $\square \times 2 = 16$

$7 \times \square = 49$ | $\square \times 4 = 16$ | $3 \times \square = 24$

$4 \times \square = 32$ | $5 \times \square = 45$ | $8 \times \square = 72$

$2 \times \square = 18$ | $\square \times 6 = 36$ | $9 \times \square = 81$

$8 \times \square = 48$ | $\square \times 9 = 63$ | $6 \times \square = 54$

Vertical Multiplication

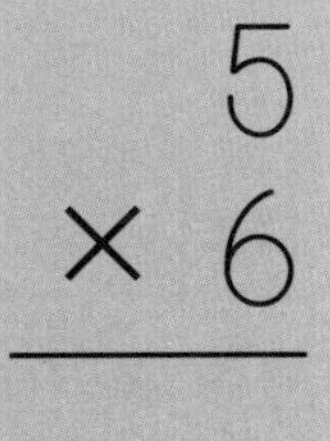

5×6	7×3	8×4	3×4	3×9	6×3
4×9	7×0	9×1	8×5	6×6	5×3
3×8	9×8	4×0	3×2	6×2	2×6
8×9	7×8	9×7	8×8	9×5	3×7
6×9	9×1	8×0	4×8	3×5	4×5

Multiplication Facts

Complete the blanks

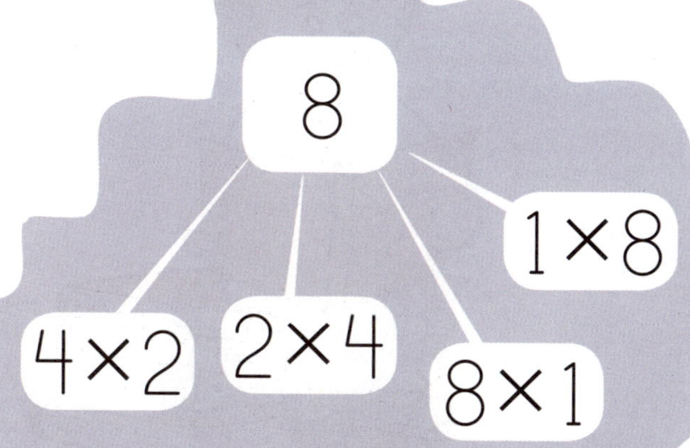

10

12

15

24

Multiplying a 2-Digit Number by a 1-Digit Number

$20 \times 3 = 2$ tens $\times 3 = 6$ tens $= 60$

$4 \times 40 = 4 \times 4$ tens $= 16$ tens $= 160$

$5 \times 30 = 5 \times 3$ tens $= 15$ tens $= 150$

$2 \times 80 = 2 \times 8$ tens $= 16$ tens $= 160$

$6 \times 20 = 6 \times 2$ tens $= 12$ tens $= 120$

$2 \times 60 = 2 \times 6$ tens $= 12$ tens $= 120$

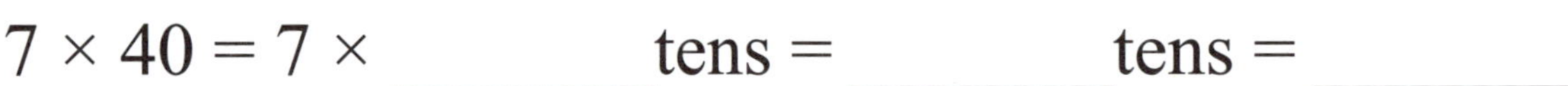

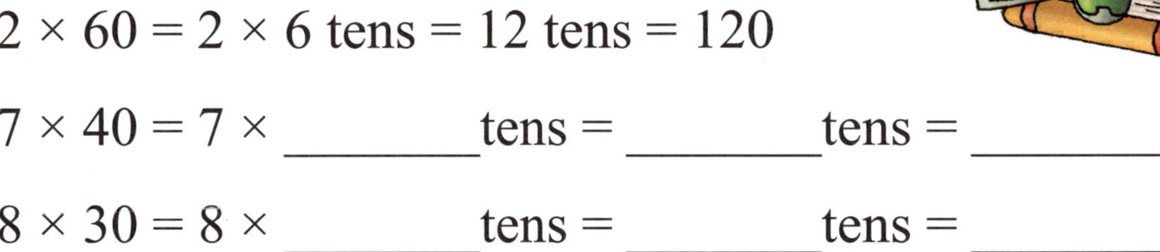

$7 \times 40 = 7 \times$ ________ tens = ________ tens = ________

$8 \times 30 = 8 \times$ ________ tens = ________ tens = ________

Fill in the boxes.

5	×	4 tens	=	200	1	×	2 tens	=	
6	×	3 tens	=		3	×	4 tens	=	
7	×	5 tens	=		5	×	3 tens	=	
3	×	9 tens	=		6	×	8 tens	=	
8	×	2 tens	=		7	×	3 tens	=	
4	×	6 tens	=		8	×	5 tens	=	

Vertical Multiplication

T O	T O	T O	T O	T O
4 0	3 0	5 0	7 0	6 0
× 3	× 6	× 4	× 8	× 5
120	180			

T O	T O	T O	T O	T O
2 0	3 0	4 0	7 0	8 0
× 7	× 9	× 2	× 2	× 9

T O	T O	T O	T O	T O
9 0	6 0	2 0	1 0	1 0
× 4	× 7	× 9	× 9	× 3

T O	T O	T O	T O	T O
5 0	3 0	6 0	8 0	6 0
× 5	× 4	× 2	× 4	× 2

Students should be encouraged to multiply mentally and put '0' in ones place.

9 Division

There are 6 oranges. We want to distribute them equally among 3 boys.

We have

3 boys

6 oranges

Gave 1 to each

3 left

We gave 1 again

No oranges

We have distributed 6 oranges equally among 3 boys. Each boy got 2 oranges.

It can be written as $6 \div 3 = 2$

If we have 15 pencils which have to be put equally in 5 boxes.

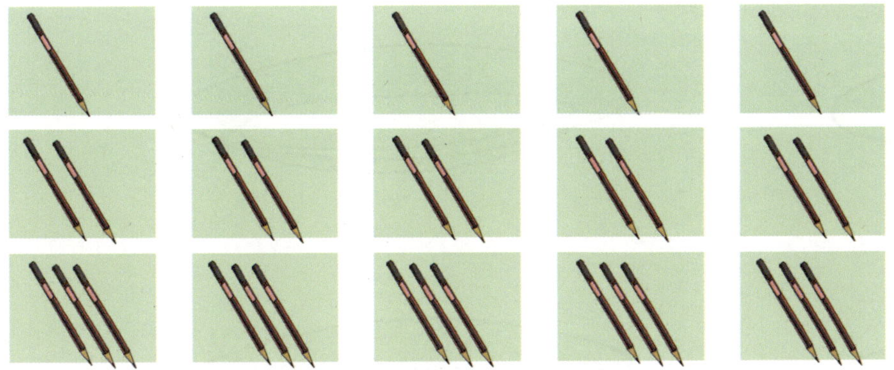

15 pencils, 1 is put in each box

1 more is put in each box (5 pencils left)

1 more is put in each box

$15 \div 5 = 3$

3 pencils will be put in each box.

Division

Lab activity

Children should work in pairs. There are 10 apples. Divide them among 2 groups, each group gets 5

$10 \div 2 = 5$

There are 12 mangoes

There are 4 plates

There are 3 mangoes in each plate.

$12 \div 4 = 3$

There are 16 cakes and 4 plates. Draw cakes on the plates so that each plate has equal number. How many in each plate?

__________ cakes

There are 18 books. There are 6 boxes. How many books can be put in each box. Draw and show the books in each box.

We write it as 18 ÷ 6 = ☐

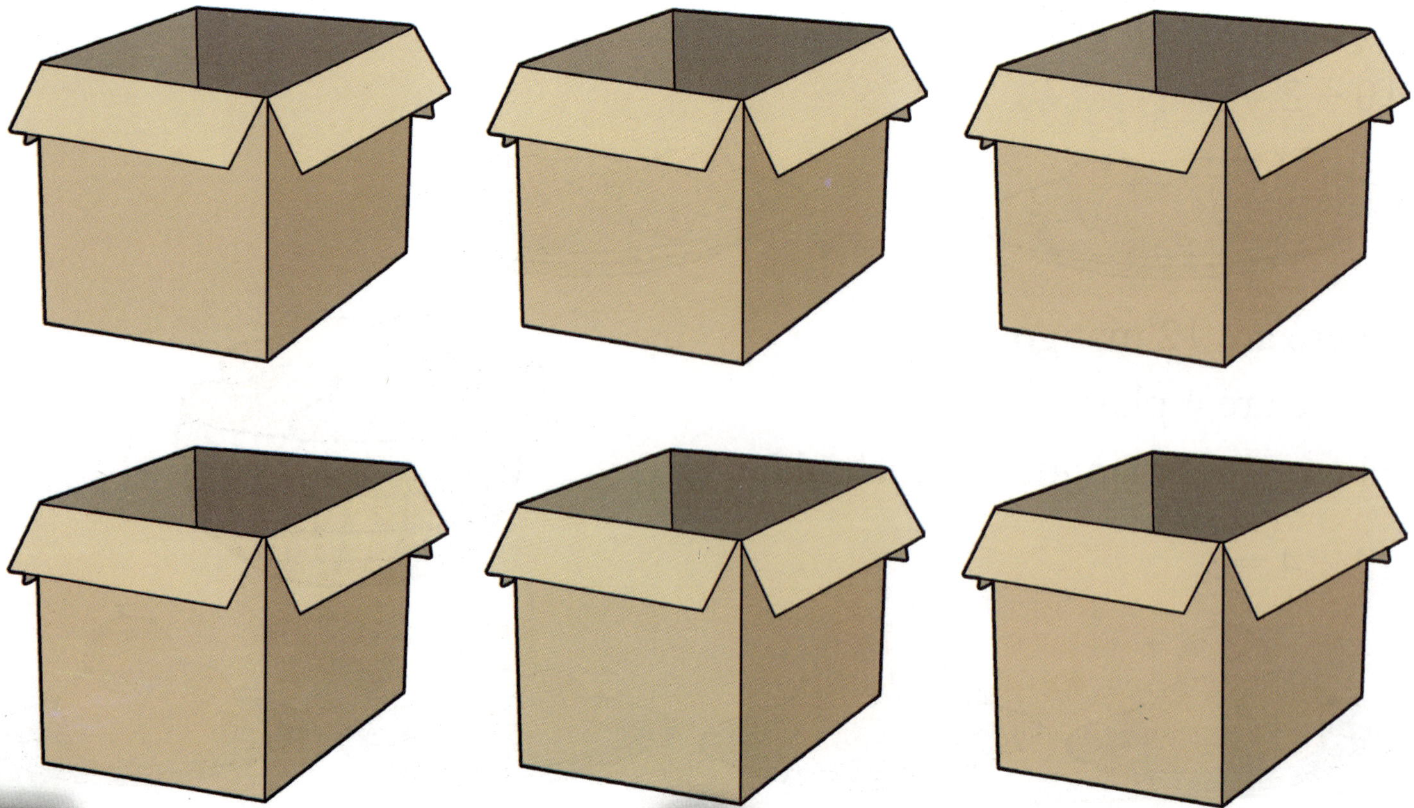

Divide into equal groups and fill in the ☐

10 bananas in 5 groups

10 ÷ 5 = 2

each groups gets ☐

8 buttons into 2 groups

8 ÷ 2 = ☐

each groups gets ☐

18 balloons in 3 groups

18 ÷ 3 = ☐

each groups gets ☐

20 cents in 4 groups

20 ÷ 4 = ☐

each groups gets ☐

16 pencils in 4 groups

16 ÷ 4 = ☐

each groups gets ☐

Division as Repeated Subtraction

Lab Activity

Students should be divided into groups of 2 or 3 and should be given beads or marbles for this activity.

Give them say 20 beads and tell them to divide into groups of 5.

The student takes away 5 and show. 20 – 5 = 15

Next 5 is taken away and put aside 15 – 5 = 10

Next 10 – 5 = 5

Next 5 – 5 = 0

There are 4 sets of 5 beads each. 20 has been divided equally into 4 sets. Each set has 5 beads.

20 ÷ 5 = 4

$$\begin{array}{r} 20 \\ -\ 5 \\ \hline 15 \\ -\ 5 \\ \hline 10 \\ -\ 5 \\ \hline 5 \\ -\ 5 \\ \hline 0 \end{array}$$

In this way within the group one child calls out the total number of beads and the number in each group. The other two find out the number of groups. Let them try these.

15 ÷ 5 = ☐ 20 ÷ 4 = ☐ 28 ÷ 7 = ☐

15 ÷ 3 = ☐ 18 ÷ 2 = ☐ 27 ÷ 3 = ☐

Division on the Number Line

Subtraction is shown by moving backwards. Repeated subtraction (division) can also be shown on number line by jumping backwards.

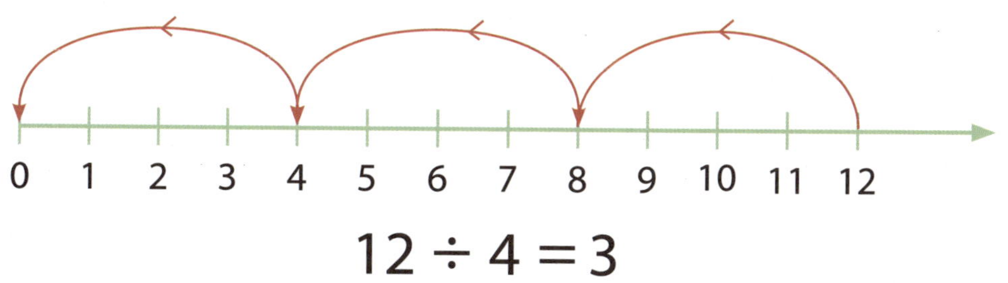

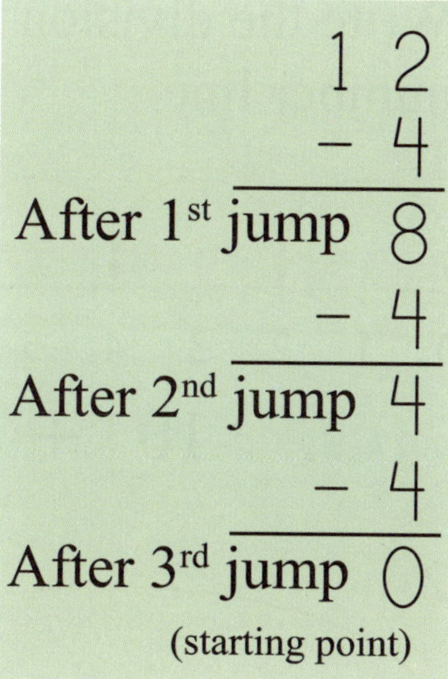

$12 \div 4 = 3$

Starting back from 12 if one jumps backward 4 steps at a time, in 3 jumps one reaches the **starting point**.

1. Show $6 \div 3$

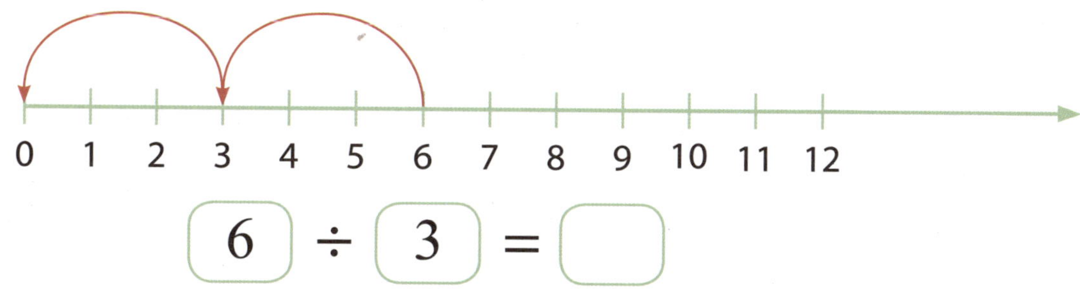

$6 \div 3 = \square$

2. Show $15 \div 3$

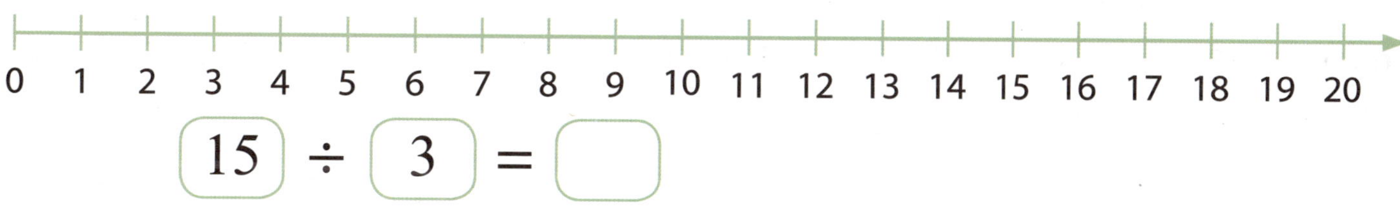

$15 \div 3 = \square$

3. Show $24 \div 6$

0 1 2 3 4 5 6 7 8 9 10 11 12 13 14 15 16 17 18 19 20 21 22 23 24

$24 \div 6 = \square$

Write the division fact for the following repeated subtraction on the number line.

1.

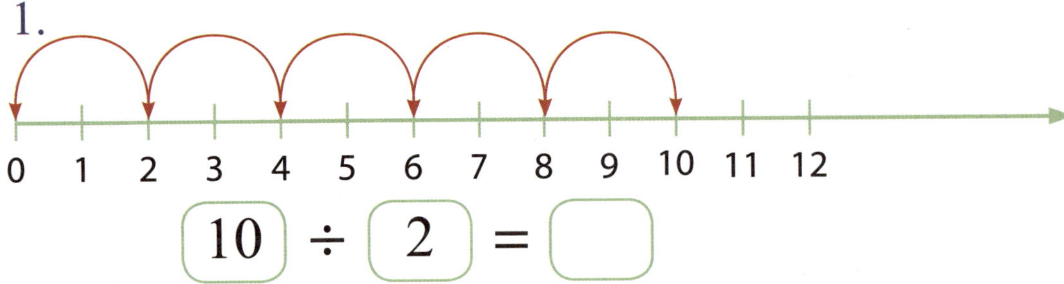

10 ÷ 2 = ☐

2.

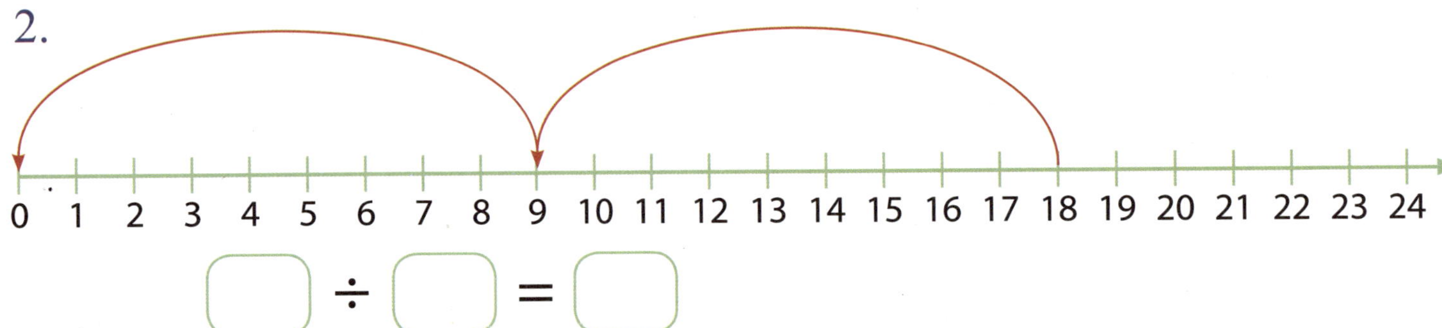

☐ ÷ ☐ = ☐

3.

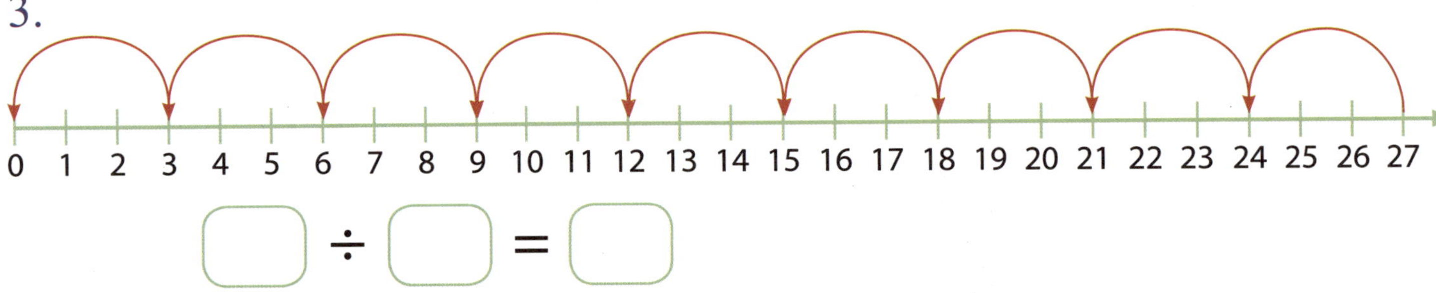

☐ ÷ ☐ = ☐

4.

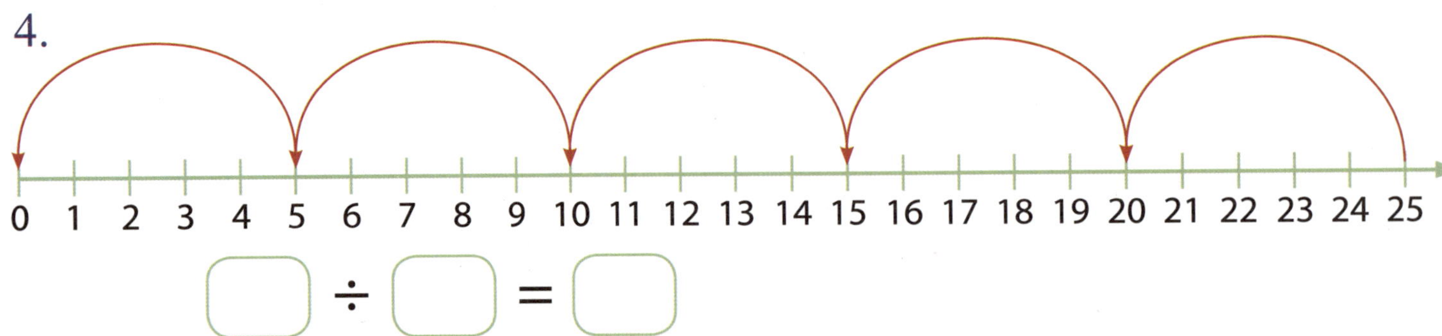

☐ ÷ ☐ = ☐

5.

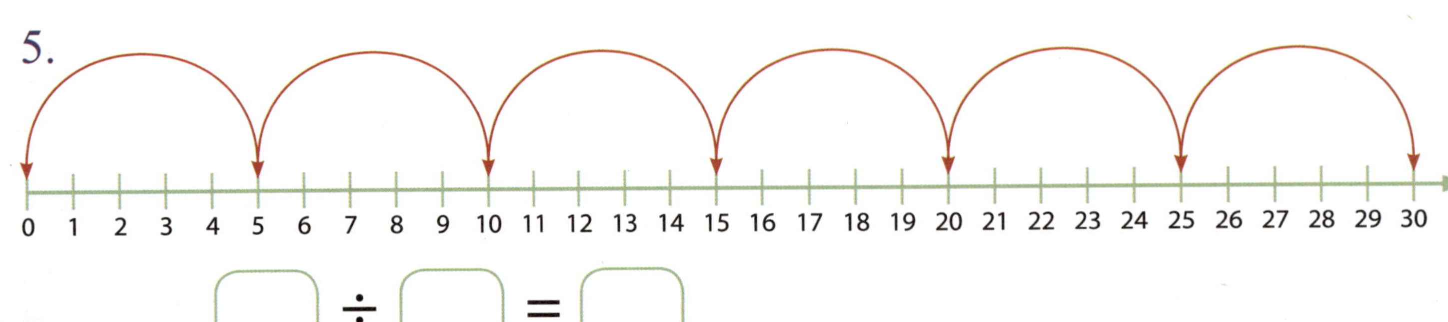

☐ ÷ ☐ = ☐

Division can be done if students know their multiplication tables thoroughly.

					Hint
18	÷	2	=	9	2 × 9 = 18
15	÷	3	=		5 × 3 = 15
20	÷	4	=		5 × 4 = 20
30	÷	5	=		
16	÷	4	=		

Write a multiplication fact for the following.

27	÷	3	=		9 × 3 = 27
36	÷	9	=		9 × 4 = 36
45	÷	5	=		
54	÷	6	=		
40	÷	10	=		
25	÷	5	=		
48	÷	8	=		

Long Division

EXAMPLE

6 ÷ 3 = 2

This can also be written as

```
             2 ←Quotient
          ________
Divisor→3 )   6 ←Dividend
             -6
            ___
              0 ←Remainder
            ___
```

8 ÷ 2 = 4

```
             4 ←Quotient
          ________
Divisor→2 )   8 ←Dividend
             -8
            ___
              0 ←Remainder
            ___
```

Find the Quotient and the Remainder

9 ÷ 3

```
       3
    ______
 3 )   9
      -9
      ___
       0
      ___
```

Q 3 R 0

12 ÷ 4

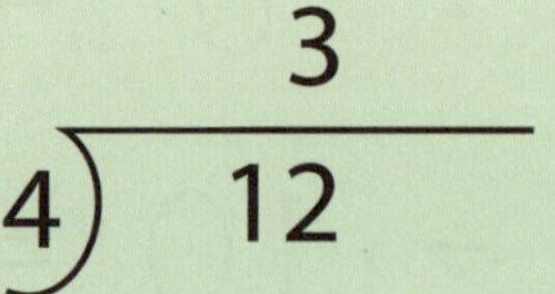

Q R

$15 \div 3$

$3\overline{)\ 15}$

Q ☐ R ☐

$20 \div 4$

$4\overline{)\ 20}$

Q ☐ R ☐

$40 \div 10$

$10\overline{)\ 40}$

Q ☐ R ☐

$36 \div 6$

$6\overline{)\ 36}$

Q ☐ R ☐

$56 \div 7$

$7\overline{)\ 56}$

Q ☐ R ☐

$64 \div 8$

$8\overline{)\ 64}$

Q ☐ R ☐

Divide

$63 \div 9$

9) 63

Q ___ R ___

$63 \div 7$

7) 63

Q ___ R ___

$49 \div 7$

7) 49

Q ___ R ___

$80 \div 10$

10) 80

Q ___ R ___

$54 \div 6$

6) 54

Q ___ R ___

$72 \div 8$

8) 72

Q ___ R ___

$56 \div 8$

8) 56

Q ___ R ___

$81 \div 9$

9) 81

Q ___ R ___

$50 \div 5$

5) 50

Q ___ R ___

Word Problems

Mini has 18 sweets. She has 6 boxes. She puts equal number of sweets in each box. How many sweets are there in each box?

18 ÷ 6 = ___ Sweets

If she has only 3 boxes. How many sweets will be there in each box?

___ ÷ ___ = ___ Sweets

A shop had 20 socks. How many boys can wear the socks?

___ ÷ ___ = ___ Boys

There are 42 buttons. A dress needs 6 buttons. On how many dresses can they be put on to?

___ ÷ ___ = ___ Dresses

There are 80 cookies. If 10 cookies are put in one packet, how many packets are needed in all?

___ ÷ ___ = ___ Packets

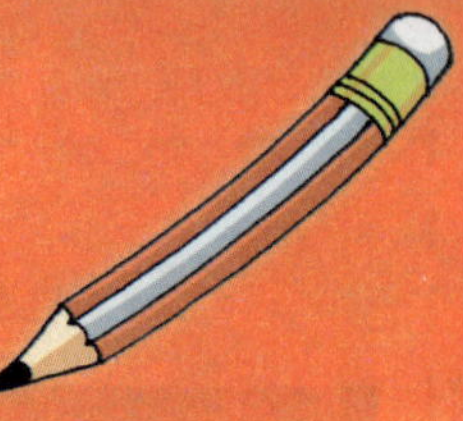

REVIEW EXERCISE 3

1. Fill in the blanks

   a. 2 times 6 = _______ + _______ = _______

   b. 5 times _____ is _____ + _____ + _____ + _____ + _____ is 35

   c. $8 \times 3 =$ _________ $\times 8 =$ _________

   d. $4 \times$ _________ $= 4 \times 2$ tens = _________

   e. $9 \times$ _______ $= 0$

   f. $24 \div$ _______ $= 4$ and _______ $\times 4 = 24$

   g. $8 \times 9 =$ _______, $72 \div$ _______ $= 8$

2. Add

594	396	478	263
+187	+278	−293	−145
____	____	____	____

3. a. Divide 28 by 4

   b. 54 by 9

5. There are 7 days in a week. How many days are there in 10 weeks?

10 Patterns

Complete the patterns given below.

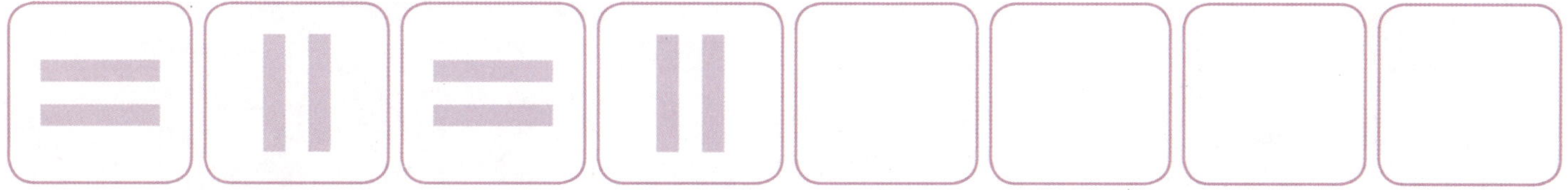

2	4	6	8				
5	10	15	20				
10	20	30	40				

10	9	8	7				
50	45	40	35				
tue	wed	thurs					
Aa	Bb	Cc	Dd				
A	B	C	D				
a	b	c	d				
+	—	+	—				
×	%	×	%				

Shapes

11

Look at things around you which look like this and draw them below these.

Cube | Sphere | Cylinder | Cone | Cuboids

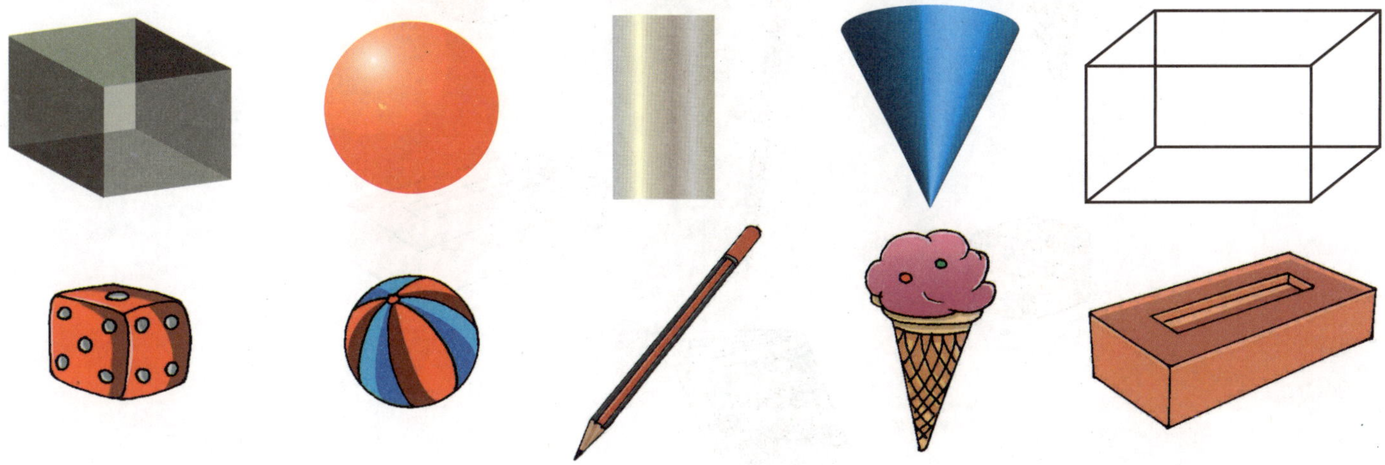

Shapes are of 2 types—flat shapes and solid shapes.

Triangle, rectangle, square, circle and oval are flat shapes.

Cubes, cylinders, cones, cuboids, spheres are solid shapes.

Triangle | Rectangle | Square | Circle | Oval

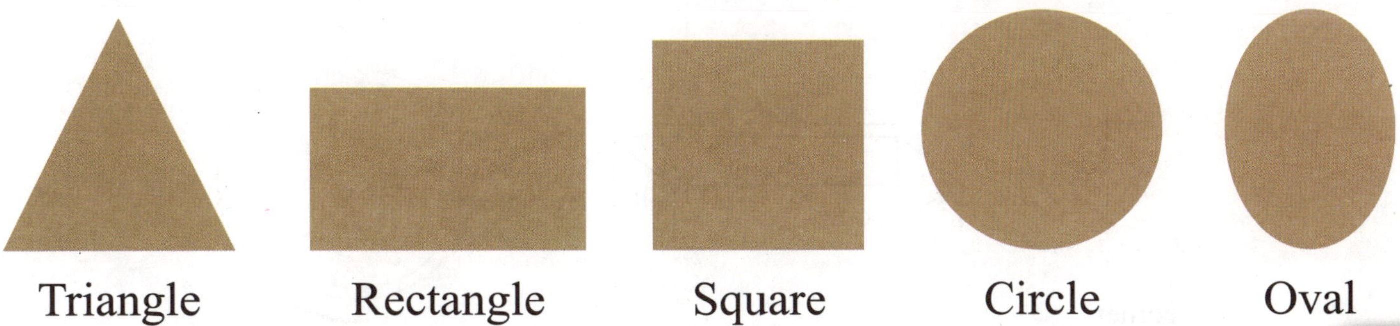

Match the objects with their shapes.

Solid shapes and flat shapes have edges, corners, surfaces.

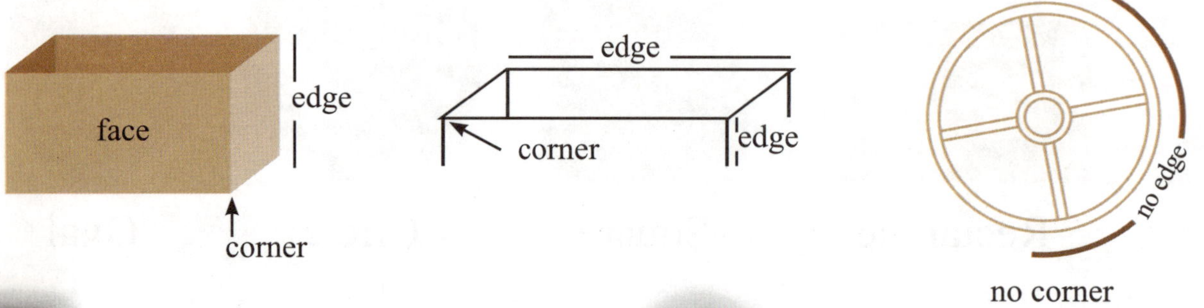

Lab Activity

1. Teacher should encourage students to bring objects like dice, erasers of different shapes to fill this table.

Name of the object	No. of corners	Straight edges	Curved edges	Flat surface	Curved surface
Dice	8	12	—	6	—
Ball					
Egg					
Pencil					
Sheet of paper					
Joker's cap					

2. The objects should be used for tracing on a sheet of paper.
   The relationship between solid objects and shapes that are traced should be shown.
3. Students should be encouraged to bring cutouts of rectangles squares, ovals, circles of different sizes and colours. Students should work in groups and make a collage using these shapes.

Straight lines and curved lines

Complete the shapes as given

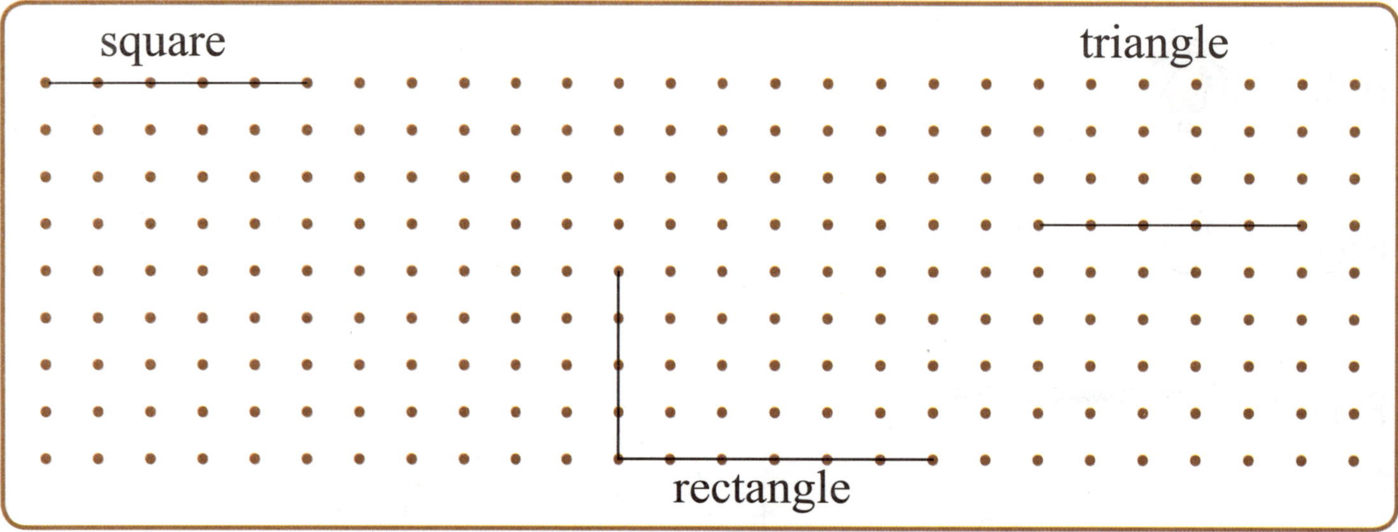

Trace straight lines in red and curved lines in green.

Money

Let us revise.

1¢

5¢

10¢

25¢

50¢

$1

$ 20

$ 50

$ 100

$ 500

$ 1000

$1 = 100 cents

Lab Activity

Rectangular and circular cards

Write $1, $2, $5, $10, $50 on rectangular cards.

Let each child make a wallet and put the paper money in it.

Ask them to fill the following table with the help of their paper money.

Article	$ 50	$ 10	$ 5	$ 2	$ 1
 $ 27		2	1	1	
 $ 46		4	1		1
 $110					
 $50					
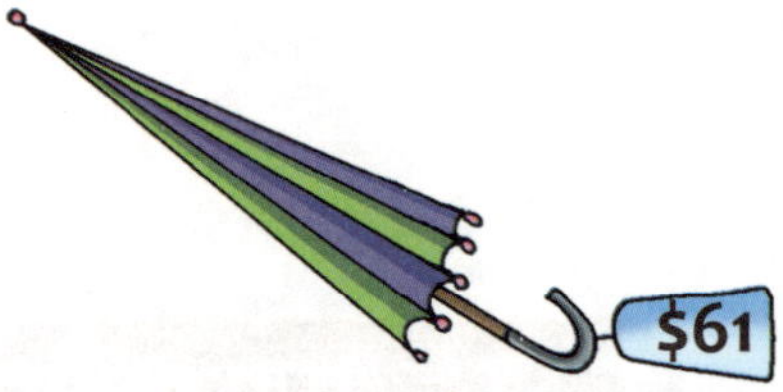 $61					
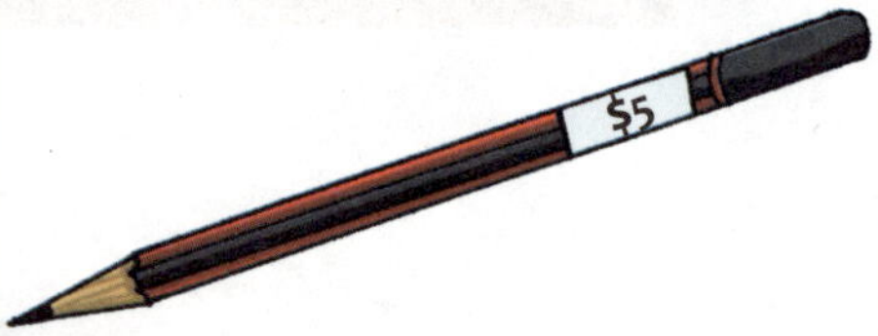 $5					

Match

UNITED STATES OF AMERICA
HALF DOLLAR

UNITED STATES OF AMERICA
FIVE D.

UNITED STATES OF AMERICA
$1

1000
FEDERAL RESERVE NOTE
THE UNITED STATES OF AMERICA
AE 77665544 B
E5
1000
ONE THOUSAND DOLLARS

10
FEDERAL RESERVE NOTE
THE UNITED STATES OF AMERICA
BL 00002040 A
L12
TEN
DOLLARS

20
FEDERAL RESERVE NOTE
THE UNITED STATES OF AMERICA
EE 23456789 A
E5
SPECIMEN
20
TWENTY DOLLARS

100
FEDERAL RESERVE NOTE
THE UNITED STATES OF AMERICA
FF 95594731 A
F6
100
ONE HUNDRED DOLLARS

UNITED STATES OF AMERICA
$1
HALF DOLLAR
FIVE D.
TEN DOLLARS

500
FEDERAL RESERVE NOTE
THE UNITED STATES OF AMERICA
B
★00000000★
500
FIVE HUNDRED DOLLARS

UNITED STATES OF AMERICA
ONE DIME
50
FEDERAL RESERVE NOTE
THE UNITED STATES OF AMERICA
AE 00067890 B
E5
50
FIFTY DOLLARS

Fill in the blanks

10 cents	+	10 cents	=	20 cents
25 cents	+	25 cents	=	☐ cents
50 cents	+	50 cents	=	☐ cents
10 cents	+	10 cents	=	☐ cents
25 cents	+	10 cents	=	☐ cents
$ 1	+	$ 1	=	$ ☐
$ 2	+	$ 2	=	$ ☐
$ 5	+	$ 2	=	$ ☐
$ 5	+	$ ☐	=	$ 10
$ 20	+	$ ☐	=	$ 25
$ 50	+	$ ☐	=	$ 100

Addition and subtraction of money

```
  2 0 cents        7 5 cents        5 0 cents
+ 2 5 cents      + 2 5 cents      + 1 0 cents
-----------      -----------      -----------

-----------      -----------      -----------
```

$$\begin{array}{r} \$10 \\ +\ \$20 \\ \hline \\ \hline \end{array}$$

$$\begin{array}{r} \$50 \\ +\ \$20 \\ \hline \\ \hline \end{array}$$

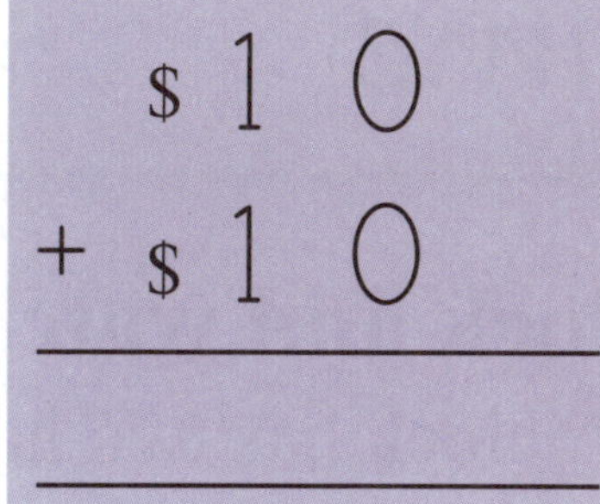

$$\begin{array}{r} \$10 \\ +\ \$10 \\ \hline \\ \hline \end{array}$$

$$\begin{array}{r} \$50 \\ -\ \$10 \\ \hline \\ \hline \end{array}$$

$$\begin{array}{r} \$25 \\ -\ \$20 \\ \hline \\ \hline \end{array}$$

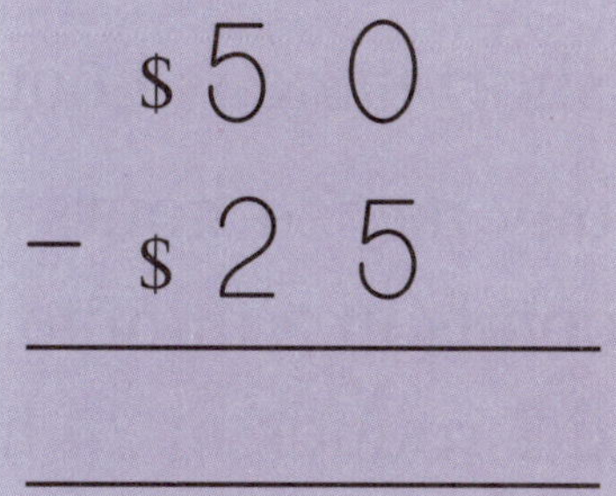

$$\begin{array}{r} \$50 \\ -\ \$25 \\ \hline \\ \hline \end{array}$$

$$\begin{array}{r} \$20 \\ -\ \$10 \\ \hline \\ \hline \end{array}$$

$$\begin{array}{r} \$35 \\ -\ \$25 \\ \hline \\ \hline \end{array}$$

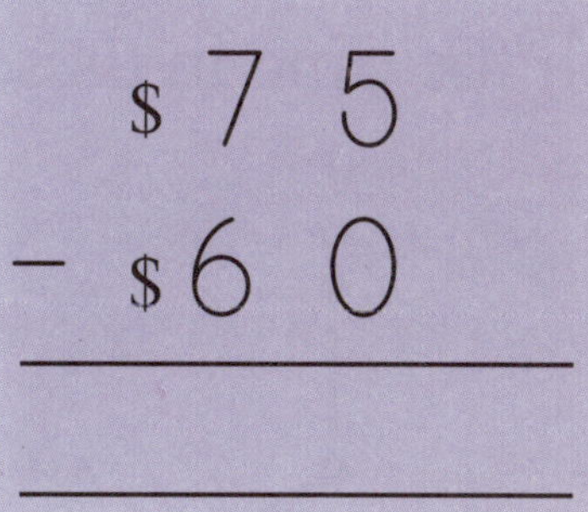

$$\begin{array}{r} \$75 \\ -\ \$60 \\ \hline \\ \hline \end{array}$$

Rosy went shopping. She saw these items with the price tags.

$ 5

$ 10

$ 15

$ 20

$ 25

$ 5

$ 30

Now help her to calculate the cost of these items.

Chips and juice	Milk and bread	Book and chips	Pen and bag
$ ____	$ ____	$ ____	$ ____
+ $ ____	+ $ ____	+ $ ____	+ $ ____
____	____	____	____

Time

13

Clock and watches tell us the time.

- A clock has two hands.
- Long hand is the minutes hand.
- Short hand is hour hand.

A day has 24 hours in a day there are 60 minutes in an hour, and 60 seconds in a minute. The short hand completes 1 full round in 12 hours and 2 rounds in 24 hours i.e. a day.

Tell the time in these clocks.

Show the time on the clock.

5 o' clock   9 o' clock   11 o' clock

Take a model of clock with moveable hands to show time.

When the hour hand is at 3 and the minute hand moves on full circle, the hour hand goes to 4.

It means one hour has passed.

In one hour there are 60 minutes.

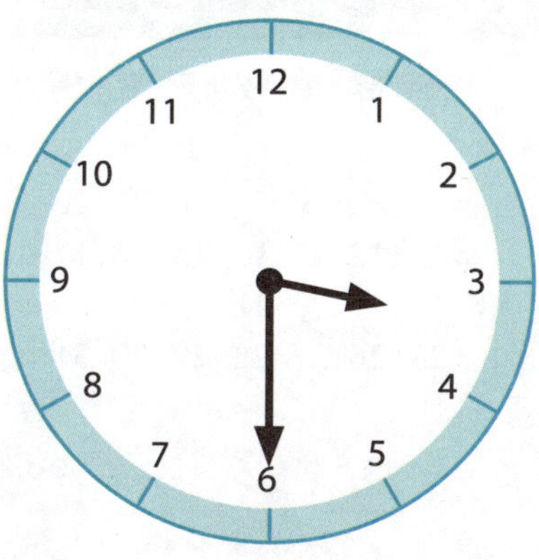

The hour hand is between 3 and 4 and the minute hand has moved is half a circle. It is at 6. It is half an hour after 3. Time is half past 3 or 3.30.

One hour = 60 minutes
Half hour = 30 minutes

Let us read the time on these clocks.

Calendar of 2016

JANUARY

S	M	T	W	T	F	S
					1	2
3	4	5	6	7	8	9
10	11	12	13	14	15	16
17	18	19	20	21	22	23
24	25	26	27	28	29	30
31						

FEBRUARY

S	M	T	W	T	F	S
	1	2	3	4	5	6
7	8	9	10	11	12	13
14	15	16	17	18	19	20
21	22	23	24	25	26	27
28	29					

MARCH

S	M	T	W	T	F	S
		1	2	3	4	5
6	7	8	9	10	11	12
13	14	15	16	17	18	19
20	21	22	23	24	25	26
27	28	29	30	31		

APRIL

S	M	T	W	T	F	S
					1	2
3	4	5	6	7	8	9
10	11	12	13	14	15	16
17	18	19	20	21	22	23
24	25	26	27	28	29	30

MAY

S	M	T	W	T	F	S
1	2	3	4	5	6	7
8	9	10	11	12	13	14
15	16	17	18	19	20	21
22	23	24	25	26	27	28
29	30	31				

JUNE

S	M	T	W	T	F	S
			1	2	3	4
5	6	7	8	9	10	11
12	13	14	15	16	17	18
19	20	21	22	23	24	25
26	27	28	29	30		

JULY

S	M	T	W	T	F	S
					1	2
3	4	5	6	7	8	9
10	11	12	13	14	15	16
17	18	19	20	21	22	23
24	25	26	27	28	29	30
31						

AUGUST

S	M	T	W	T	F	S
	1	2	3	4	5	6
7	8	9	10	11	12	13
14	15	16	17	18	19	20
21	22	23	24	25	26	27
28	29	30	31			

SEPTEMBER

S	M	T	W	T	F	S
				1	2	3
4	5	6	7	8	9	10
11	12	13	14	15	16	17
18	19	20	21	22	23	24
25	26	27	28	29	30	

OCTOBER

S	M	T	W	T	F	S
						1
2	3	4	5	6	7	8
9	10	11	12	13	14	15
16	17	18	19	20	21	22
23	24	25	26	27	28	29
30	31					

NOVEMBER

S	M	T	W	T	F	S
		1	2	3	4	5
6	7	8	9	10	11	12
13	14	15	16	17	18	19
20	21	22	23	24	25	26
27	28	29	30			

DECEMBER

S	M	T	W	T	F	S
				1	2	3
4	5	6	7	8	9	10
11	12	13	14	15	16	17
18	19	20	21	22	23	24
25	26	27	28	29	30	31

Look at the calendar and circle your Birthday in blue.

Today in Green.

Your Mother's birthday in Pink

Your best friend's birthday in yellow.

Ask your partner's birthday – circle it in purple.

Ask your teacher's birthday – circle in orange.

Tell the days, these birthdays fall on ______________________________

See the calendar and fill in the blanks.

1. There are _________ days in a week.
2. _________ is the first day of the January.
3. There are _________ months in a year.
4. In March, there are _________ days.
5. June has _________ days.
6. _________ has less days than other months.
7. The eighth month of the year is _________
8. This is the month of _________
9. There are _________ Mondays in May.
10. Universal Children's Day (20th Nov.) falls on _________
11. My school reopens on first Monday in the month of July. The date is _________
12. 3 days after 20th April is _________ (date)
13. 7 days after 12th May is _________ (date)
14. 1 day before 1st July is _________ (day)
15. We have autumn break for 10 days from last Friday of September. We have holidays from _________ September to _________ October.

There are 12 months in a year. Write their names.

Puzzle on week

Sun	Mon	Tue	Wed	Thu	Fri	Sat
		1	2	3	4	5
						12
						19
						26
			30			

What is the date of each activity?

1. Rob goes for a movie on the first weekend of the month.

   ____

2. He watches a football match on the first Wed of the month.

   ____

3. He goes for a birthday party 2 weeks after the match.

   ____

4. Cricket practice is 2 days after the party.

   ____

5. Skating practice is every Friday evening.

   ___________ ___________ ___________ ___________

Mass

14

Man is heavier

Ball is lighter

Circle the heavier object.

Here we could say by comparison

Put objects on the scale.

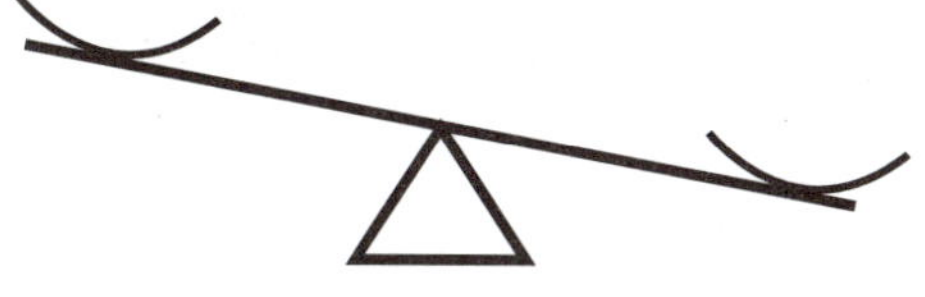

More about weight

Here a shopkeeper is weighing fruits with a I kilogram weight. Some commonly used big weights.

Some commonly used small weights.

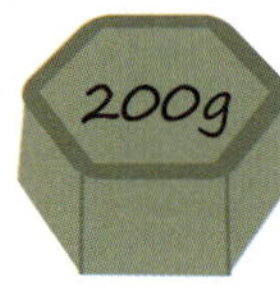

50 grams is written as 50g, 100 grams as 100g. Short form of grams is g.

Write down the weights in these cases.

1 kg + 1 kg = 2 kg

1 kg

Flour = ☐

Fishes = ☐

Write 'more than', 'less than' or 'equal to' in the blanks.

The weight of oil bottle is

__________ 1kg

The weight of the sack of potatoes is __________ 1kg

The weight of the box is

__________ 1kg

The weight of turnips is

__________ 1kg

Grams is the unit for lighter objects.

1 kg = 1000 grams

Write the weights

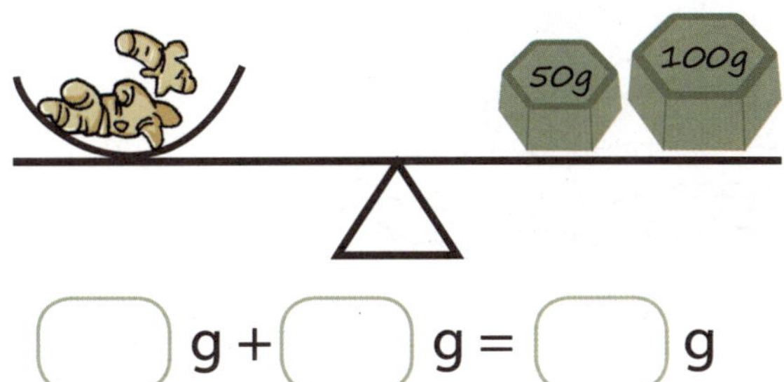

☐ g + ☐ g = ☐ g

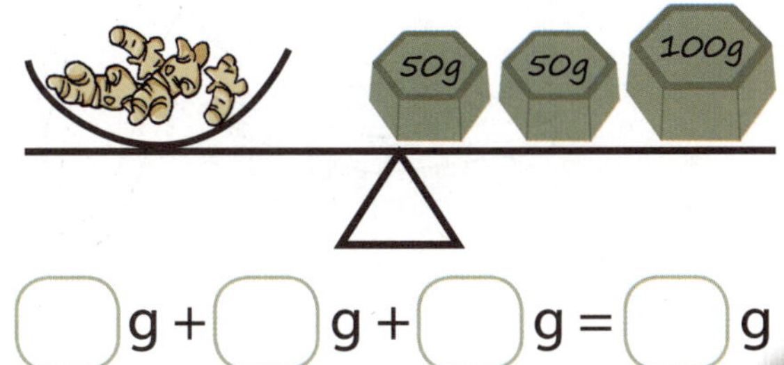

☐ g + ☐ g + ☐ g = ☐ g

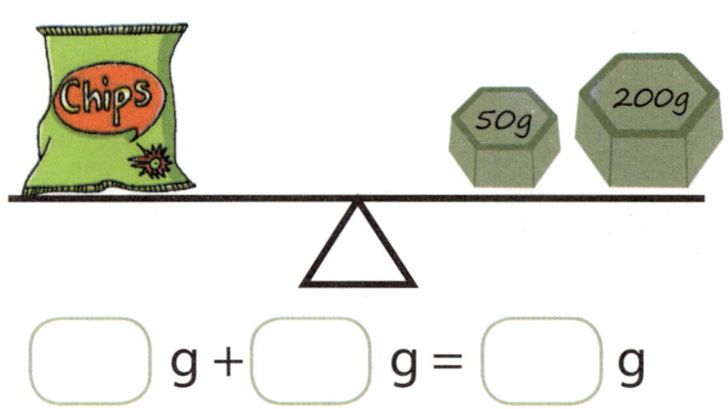

□ g + □ g = □ g

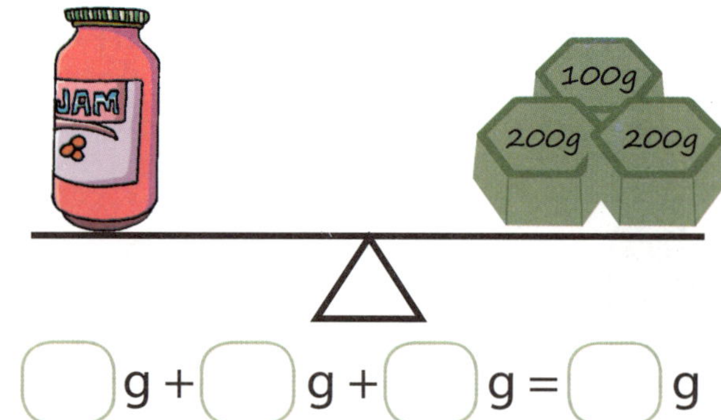

□ g + □ g + □ g = □ g

Lab Activity

Make a list of …

1. Things weighing less than a kg. ______ ______ ______ ______
2. Things weighing more than a kg. ______ ______ ______ ______
3. Different types of balances seen around you. ________ ________
4. Collect packets or labels showing weight of different objects.

Measurement

15

Long and Short

For measuring we sometimes use parts of our body like

handspan cubit a foot span

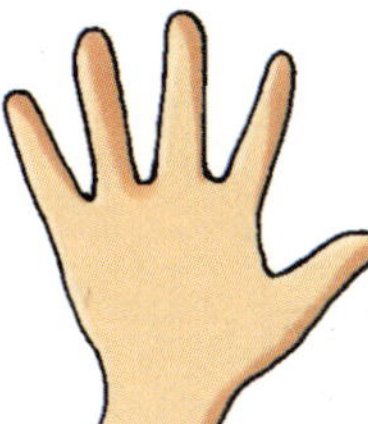

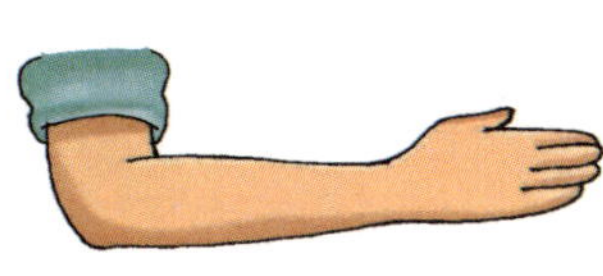

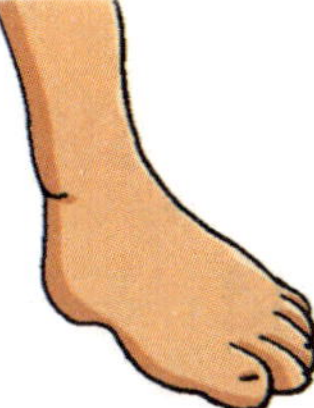

These are **non-standard units of measurement**.

A ruler or a scale has a standard unit.

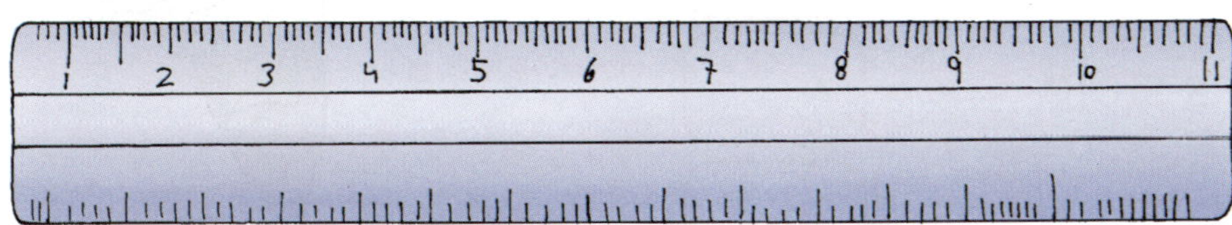

The pencil is ____________ centimetres long.

The brush is ____________ centimetres long.

The spoon is ____________ centimetres long.

The pencil box is ____________ centimetres long.

The eraser is about ____________ centimetres long.

How long is a metre?

1 metre = 100 cm

Centimetre is used for small measurements. To find how far is the playground from the classroom, we use metre.

A bedsheet is more than 2 metres long. Your desk is about a metre long.

Which of these will be in centimetre or metre.

1. Width of computer screen
2. Height of a 1 year old child
3. Length of a banana
4. Length of your arm
5. Length of your mother's stole
6. Length of a nail
7. Height of your classroom

1. The eraser is 1 cm long
   length of 3 erasers = 1+1+1=3 cm

2. 4 crayons = 2+2+2+2+2=8 cm

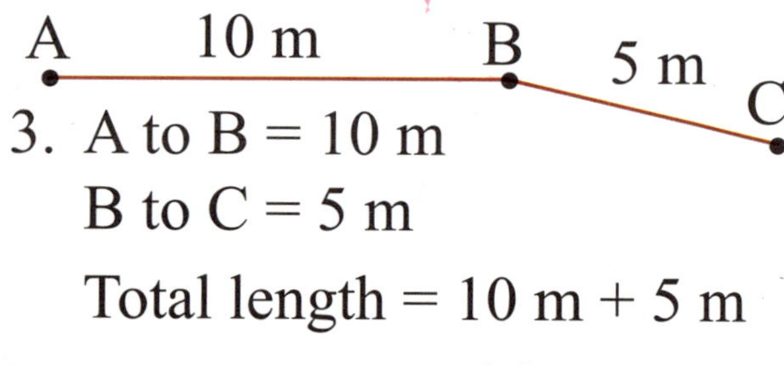

3. A to B = 10 m
   B to C = 5 m
   Total length = 10 m + 5 m
   = 15 m

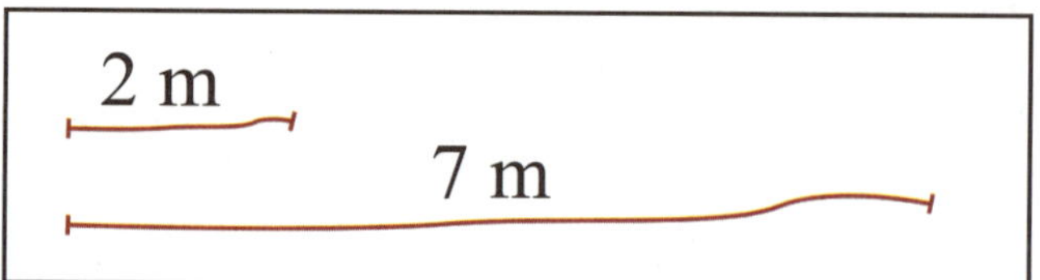

4. The total length of rope is –
   2 m + 7 m = 9 m

Capacity

16

Colour the vessel which will hold less water in blue.

Liquids like– water, milk, oil are measured in litres and millilitres.

Capacity of a bottle of cold drink is 500 mL.

Pack of juice is 200 mL

Normal bucket is about 8 L

Bottle of water 1 L

Small containers' capacity is in milliliters or mL
Large containers' capacity is in litres of L
Choose 'L' or 'mL' for

	L	mL
Water tank	✓	✗
Coca cola bottle (big)		
Bottle of medicine		
Water bottle		
Petrol for cars		

Capacity of a bottle  = 4 glasses

Capacity of a bucket  = ☐ glasses

Capacity of a drum  = ☐ glasses

17 Data-Handling

Representation of Data

The teacher asked the students about the books they read.

She recorded the information like this.

Number of books or comics read in a week

Alisha	Arthur	Mary	Sam	Monika	Rezwan	Arnold

Answer the following

1. ___________ reads the most
2. ___________ read more comics than Sam.
3. ___________ read less comics than Arthur.
4. ___________ read two more books than Rezwan.

Presentation of Data

Observe the information collected

Number of front teeth broken

Number of teeth broken	0	1	2
Students			

Now answer the following questions if is one student

1. How many students have last 2 front teeth? __________
2. How many students did not lose any tooth? __________
3. How many students lost one tooth? __________
4. How many students lost 3 teeth? __________

Attendance sheet for February 3

Class II	Number of students	Number absent
A	32	2
B	37	5
C	35	0
D	40	4
E	38	1

Answer the following

1. ____________ students from class II were absent on 3 Feb.
2. In ____________ all the students were present.
3. The class with highest number of absent students is ____________
4. ____________ students were present in II E on Feb 3

My favourite milk shake

Picture	Name of the fruit	No. of students
	Mango	5
	Banana	8
	Sapodilla	3
	Chocolate	12
	Vanilla	2
	Strawberry	10

Answer the following

1. The favourite shake is ____________

2. ____________ students like mango shake.

3. ____________ flavour is least liked by students.

4. Only 10 students like ____________ shake.

Activity

Let the students make a list of 10 students of their class. They will write their birth dates next to their names, (like 12 January, 18 November) Then they will arrange from January to December.

Sr. No.	Name	Birthday

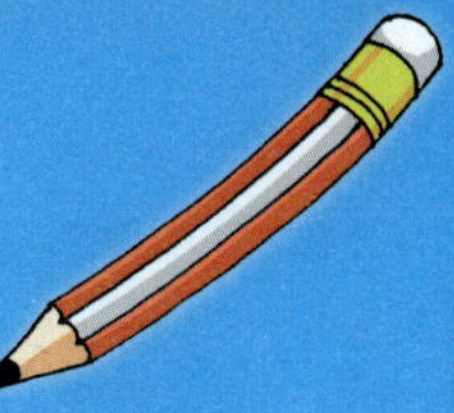

REVIEW EXERCISE 4

1. Fill in the blanks

   a. $ 1 ________ cents.

   b. ________ ¢ + ________ ¢ = $ 1

   c. ________ comes after July.

   d. March comes before ________

   e. Capacity of a table spoon is measured in ________ (L/mL)

   f. Weight of an eraser is written in ________ (kg/g)

2. What time is it?

3. Draw the hands of the clock to show the time.

Half past 8

Half past 2

4. Cost of 1 pencil is $ 5. What is the cost of 8 such pencils?

5. Now write the shape of the following objects

    c. A tube light ___________

    d. A book ___________

    e. A match box ___________

    f. The moon ___________

6. These items are to be packed in 4 bags given below.
   Each bag should not have more than 6 kg. Write or draw how you will pack each bag (all items have to be packed).